T0357867

# PRAISE FOR *EVERY THOUGHT CAPTIVE*

*Every Thought Captive* is a powerful guide for anyone struggling with the chaos of their own mind. Kyle Idleman masterfully combines Scripture, personal experience, and practical strategies to help readers take control of their thoughts and experience true transformation. If you're ready to break free from mental strongholds, this book is for you.

**CRAIG GROESCHEL,** pastor, Life.
Church; author, *The Benefit of Doubt*

Changed thoughts make for changed lives. In *Every Thought Captive*, Kyle Idleman does a masterful job of weaving practical wisdom with biblical revelation, all while offering real-life application. I found myself circling paragraphs and noting pages to share. This book won't change just your life; it will change the lives of those you pass it to.

**KELLY BALARIE,** author, *Take Every Thought Captive*; speaker; blogger at www.purposefulfaith.com

It can be frustrating to fall into cycles of negative thoughts and feel stuck. Kyle Idleman knows this all too well, but he also knows that the power of right thinking can change everything. Let his biblical guidance and time-tested experience show you how to renew your mind and set your heart on things above.

**MARK BATTERSON,** *New York Times* bestselling author, *The Circle Maker*

This book illustrates why I try to read everything Kyle Idleman writes. It's fresh, practical, encouraging, convicting, and challenging. I'm a better person when I apply biblical principles to my life, and Kyle helps me do exactly that. Read this book, and let Kyle guide you on a journey of discovery and transformation. Renew your mind and change your life!

**LEE STROBEL,** bestselling author, *The Case for Christ* and *Seeing the Supernatural*

Our modern moment seems unable to recognize the spiritual significance of what we put in front of our eyes. This book is a welcome reminder that the Bible assumes we have agency in what we put in front of our minds, and that these choices affect how (or what!) we believe. Though this is perhaps easier said than done, *Every Thought Captive* is a great practical guide on how to start.

**JUSTIN WHITMEL EARLEY,** business
lawyer; author, *Habits of the Household*

I've heard it said that our emotions are like smoke from the fire of our hearts. If you notice smoke in your house, don't focus on the smoke; find the fire! Kyle Idleman contends that too many of us attempt to fix the "smoke" in our lives with behavior modification when what we really need is a gospel encounter in the depth of our souls. This book will help you so much. Pastor Kyle is one of our generation's best communicators. Insightful, relatable, inspiring, and circumspect—he has it all.

**J. D. GREEAR,** PhD, pastor,
The Summit Church

In our efforts to grow, change, break old habits, improve relationships, and become more Christlike, we so often begin at the wrong place. Good intentions and willpower certainly have their place, but Kyle Idleman takes us to the source of where real change happens—our thinking. In Kyle's personal and sensitive style, he takes us on a biblical and practical journey to learn how changing our thinking changes our lives.

**CHIP INGRAM,** CEO and teaching pastor,
Living on the Edge; author, *True Spirituality*

I love the "Kyle style"—true spiritual depth with true readability and approachability. And this book is absolutely spot-on about the most important thing any of us can offer—our attention. I'm so glad he's writing about this.

**BRANT HANSEN,** radio host; bestselling
author, *Unoffendable* and *The Men We Need*

# EVERY THOUGHT CAPTIVE

# EVERY THOUGHT CAPTIVE

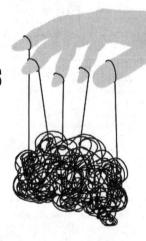

CALM THE MENTAL CHAOS
THAT KEEPS YOU STUCK,
DRAINS YOUR HOPE,
AND HOLDS YOU BACK

# KYLE IDLEMAN

ZONDERVAN
BOOKS

ZONDERVAN BOOKS

*Every Thought Captive*
Copyright © 2025 by Kyle Idleman

Published in Grand Rapids, Michigan, by Zondervan. Zondervan is a registered trademark of The Zondervan Corporation, L.L.C., a wholly owned subsidiary of HarperCollins Christian Publishing, Inc.

Requests for information should be addressed to customercare@harpercollins.com.

Zondervan titles may be purchased in bulk for educational, business, fundraising, or sales promotional use. For information, please email SpecialMarkets@Zondervan.com.

ISBN 978-0-310-36992-9 (international trade paper edition)

Library of Congress Cataloging-in-Publication Data

Names: Idleman, Kyle, author.
Title: Every thought captive : calm the mental chaos that keeps you stuck, drains your hope, and holds you back / Kyle Idleman.
Description: Grand Rapids, Michigan : Zondervan Books, [2025] | Includes bibliographical references.
Identifiers: LCCN 2024058211 (print) | LCCN 2024058212 (ebook) | ISBN 9780310364030 (hardcover) | ISBN 9780310364047 (ebook) | ISBN 9780310364054 (audio)
Subjects: LCSH: Self-actualization (Psychology)—Religious aspects—Christianity. | Christian life. | BISAC: RELIGION / Christian Living / Personal Growth | SELF-HELP / Motivational & Inspirational
Classification: LCC BV4598.2 .I35 2025 (print) | LCC BV4598.2 (ebook) | DDC 248/.4—dc23/eng/20250114
LC record available at https://lccn.loc.gov/2024058211
LC ebook record available at https://lccn.loc.gov/2024058212

Published in association with Don Gates of the literary agency The Gates Group, www.the-gates-group.com.

*Cover design: Curt Diepenhorst*
*Cover illustration: OnlyFlags / Shutterstock*
*Interior design: Denise Froehlich*

*Printed in the United States of America*

25 26 27 28 29 LBC 5 4 3 2 1

*To my son and sons-in-law—*
*men who understand that the greatest battles*
*are fought in the quiet chambers of the mind,*
*and the noblest victories won in moments*
*no one else can see.*
*In you, I see the brave surrender of men*
*who have learned that strength flows*
*from yielding every thought to Jesus.*

# CONTENTS

O ver the years, I've walked alongside countless individuals desperate for transformation. Their stories, while unique, often share a common thread of frustration and discouragement. Here are just three examples.

Jacque, a young professional, is battling anxiety that threatens to derail her career. Despite years of undergoing therapy and reading self-help books, she still finds herself paralyzed by racing thoughts and worst-case scenarios.

Mark, a recovering addict, has been clean for months but constantly fears relapse. He has been down this path so many times before, and more than anything, he wants this time to be different. His mind seems to wage war against him, replaying memories of past failures and tempting him into old patterns.

Helen, a mother of three, struggles with anger issues that have stretched her family relationships to the breaking point. She promised herself she would do things differently than her mother, but she seems unable to break the cycle and feels powerless against the surge of emotions that control her words and actions.

These stories represent a universal human struggle. All of us, at some point, find ourselves at war with our own minds. We know what we want to do and who we want to be, but our thoughts seem to have a will of their own. Every reader of this book, and the author as well, knows the reality of this struggle.

While this internal battle is real, it is not new. The apostle Paul wrote about it nearly two thousand years ago: "We demolish arguments and every pretension that sets itself up against the knowledge of God, and we take captive every thought to make it obedient to Christ" (2 Corinthians 10:5). But in our modern world of constant distraction and information overload, this ancient wisdom has never been more relevant—or more challenging to apply.

That's why I've written this book. Through years of pastoral counseling, diving deep into Scripture, and my own personal journey, I've discovered that the key to lasting transformation lies not in behavior modification or willpower alone, but in learning to take our thoughts captive.

The stakes couldn't be higher. Our thoughts shape our emotions, drive our actions, and ultimately determine the course of our lives. Left unchecked, they can lead us down paths of destruction or, at best, stagnation and mediocrity. But when we learn to harness the power of our minds, aligning our thoughts with God's truth, we unlock the potential for profound change and abundant living.

What's particularly exciting is that modern neuroscience is catching up to what the Bible has been teaching for millennia. For centuries, the human brain was believed to be a fixed, unchangeable organ. However, recent research has shattered this misconception, revealing the brain's astounding capacity for change—a phenomenon known as neuroplasticity. This scientific discovery aligns perfectly with the biblical concept of mind renewal, as expressed in Romans 12:2: "Do not conform to the pattern of this world, but be transformed by the renewing of your mind."

This convergence of scriptural wisdom and neuroscientific discovery offers us unprecedented hope and practical strategies for personal transformation. As you embark on this journey of taking your thoughts captive, you're not merely reading a book or even engaging in a spiritual exercise; you're actively reshaping the physical structure of your brain.

In the pages that follow, we'll explore biblically grounded and scientifically verified strategies for:

- identifying toxic thought patterns
- interrupting negative mental loops
- replacing lies with truth
- harnessing the power of neuroplasticity for lasting change
- implementing practical daily habits to reinforce healthy thought patterns
- leveraging the supernatural connection between thoughts, emotions, and physical well-being
- cultivating a mindset that leads to true peace, joy, and purpose

This isn't just another self-help book; it's an invitation to a radical rewiring of your mind—that has the power to transform every aspect of your life. Whether you're battling anxiety like Jacque, fighting addiction like Mark, struggling with anger like Helen, or facing any other mental stronghold, this book, through the wisdom of Scripture and the power of the Holy Spirit, offers a road map to freedom.

I'm going to make a promise based on Romans 12:2: If you commit to the principles and practices outlined in these pages, you will experience a renewed mind and a transformed life. You'll develop the ability to not just react to life's circumstances but to proactively shape your reality through the power of intentional thinking.

Are you ready to take every thought captive and step into the life you were meant to live? Let's begin this journey together.

# THE POWER OF OUR THOUGHTS

*Do not be conformed . . .*

**O**ur minds are being molded.
Every moment of every day, whether we realize it or not, our thoughts are being shaped by forces both seen and unseen. The shows we watch, the social media we scroll through, the conversations we have, the memories we revisit—all of these experiences are literally wiring our brains, forming neural pathways that will determine how we think, feel, and live.

This isn't just ancient wisdom or modern psychology; it's actually both. The apostle Paul wrote about it two thousand years ago when he warned us to "not conform to the pattern of this world." Today, neuroscientists can observe this conforming process happening in our brains through neuroplasticity—our brain's ability to be reshaped by repeated thoughts and experiences.

In the chapters ahead, we'll explore three fundamental truths about the power of our thoughts: First, we'll discover how our minds are constantly being molded, whether we're aware of it or not. We'll see how the things we think about most deeply shape who we become. Second, we'll examine the law of cognition—how our thoughts create beliefs, which generate emotions, which drive behaviors, which ultimately determine our lives. Finally, we'll uncover the rule of exposure—how what we allow ourselves to be exposed to becomes the raw material for our thoughts and the blueprint for our lives.

Understanding these principles isn't just an academic exercise; it's essential for anyone who wants to break free from destructive thought patterns and experience true transformation. Because here's the reality—either you will take your thoughts captive or your thoughts will take you captive.

CHAPTER 1

# MIND MOLDING

## WHATEVER SHAPES YOUR
## BRAIN SHAPES YOUR LIFE

Have you ever paused to consider how much of your life is shaped by your thoughts? The struggles you face, the emotions that overwhelm you, the habits you can't seem to break, the relationship drama that wears you out—all of these have their roots in your mind.

Think about it. The recurring anxiety that keeps you up at night? It starts with a thought. The relationship conflicts that leave you feeling drained and misunderstood? They're fueled by thought patterns. The spiritual stagnation you can't seem to shake? It's rooted in your stagnant thoughts. Even that goal you've been chasing for years but can't seem to reach—your thoughts are likely playing a significant role.

If you could transform your thinking, how would your life change? If the mental narratives holding you back were replaced with biblical thoughts of hope, confidence, and purpose, how would it begin to mold your life? The truth is, your life is being molded right now, in this very moment, by your thoughts. The question is, are you actively participating in that molding, or are you letting it happen by default?

In this chapter, we're going to dive deep into the principle of mind molding. We'll explore how our thoughts shape our reality and understand why it's so vital to learn to take each thought captive.

I want to begin this exploration with a story that requires a quick disclaimer: *Neither my wife nor I promote or sell marijuana or marijuana-related paraphernalia.*

With that out of the way, let me tell you what happened a few years ago. My wife received Christmas cookie molds. As a Christmas gift. On Christmas day. (Which is kind of like giving celebratory diapers to a toddler who just became potty-trained or a bicycle to a sixteen-year-old who just got a driver's license.)

We put the Christmas cookie molds into deep storage, aka the kitchen drawer where we keep other cookware and miscellaneous items that we can't bring ourselves to get rid of. Like the pair of oven mitts that read, "Resentment is my secret ingredient."

As Christmas approached the following year, we decided to get into the Christmas spirit by making some Christmas cookies for our neighbors and the local nursing home residents. My wife remembered the Christmas cookie molds and dug them out of the drawer, trusting that their lovely leafy shapes would all somehow celebrate the Christmas season.

When I got home, a sampling of the Christmas cookies was set out on our kitchen island, and I immediately recognized what my innocent and virtuous wife failed to realize—she had made dozens of marijuana leaf–shaped cookies to celebrate the birth of our Lord and Savior.

And that's how I almost became the pastor who passed out marijuana Christmas cookies to his neighbors and nursing home residents as a way to celebrate the incarnation.

There was a brief moment of panic as I tried to confirm that no weed-shaped Christmas cookies had been disbursed. I was imagining a news story with cameras in front of the nursing home. I subconsciously started to prepare my defense:

## We didn't know!
## It wasn't intentional.
## It was just a mold someone gave us.

My defense would be true, but regardless of our intention or awareness, the mold *was* a marijuana leaf. And of course, our cookies would come out in the shape they were molded in. That's how molds work.

Molds have power—they cause things to take their shape, and it never works the other way around—but like my wife and me with the marijuana leaf mold, we don't pay much attention to the molds we are given that end up shaping our lives, governing our emotions, regulating our relationships, and determining our future.

## SQUEEZED

It may sound obvious, but the most important thing about you is who you are becoming. I love how the brilliant Christian philosopher Dallas Willard said it: "Your life is the person you're becoming, and we so often think of our life in terms of our accomplishments, but I think that's a very tragic mistake. What you get out of your life and what God gets out of your life is the person you become."[1]

Yet for most of us, who we are becoming is something that just *happens*. We don't really think about it. That's what it means to be "molded." We are shaped by things beyond our control. The shape of our lives is something that *happens* to us.

We may assume who we are becoming is determined by our intentions. When our lives aren't what we had hoped they'd be, we let ourselves off the hook because we know our intentions were good. But our lives are not molded by good intentions. Chances are you had intentions of being a certain kind of person, or maybe of *not* being a certain kind of person. You had ideas about the man or woman, the husband or wife, the father or mother, the follower of Jesus you would become. So is that who you are?

I want to ask you to do something you're probably not going to want to do. In just a moment I'm going to ask you to set this book down, go find a mirror, and look at yourself for at least a minute while thinking about two incredibly important questions:

### Who am I becoming?
### Is this who I want to be?

The reason I know you probably won't do this little exercise is that I know me. If I had just started reading a book and was told to set it down and go stare at myself in the mirror while asking myself some existential questions, I would either roll my eyes and keep reading or assume I already know the answers to these questions. But if we are going to understand how our lives have been shaped by our thoughts, we need to be honest about the shape our lives are in. So take a moment, set this book down, go look in the mirror, and think about these two questions: *Who am I becoming? Is this who I want to be?*

Okay, go ahead and do it.

*Did you do it?* If you did, then you can skip this next paragraph. *Still reading?* Not surprised. Look, this book about thinking is going to challenge you to stop and think about some things. Part of our problem is that we have allowed our minds to be *consumers* rather than *processors*. If you consume this content without thinking, you will have missed the point.

So here's what I'm going to do for you readers who want to get through several pages every time you sit down to read: I'll provide a number of places where you'll find several blank lines so you can stop reading and do what I like to call "thought thinking." That's when you stop, and without any distractions, think about your thoughts. The more challenging this is for you, the more you need to do it.

The average reader takes 1.7 minutes to read one page. Based on the reasonable assumption that my readers are above average, I'm going to round that down to 1.5 minutes. That means by giving you blank lines in places along the way, I'm giving you three minutes to practice taking your thoughts captive. So whenever you come to these blank spaces, it's time to practice your thought thinking.

Let's try it again. Go look at yourself in the mirror, take three minutes, and think through those two questions: *Who am I becoming? Is this who I want to be?*

_____

_____

_____

_____

_____

_____

_____

_____

_____

_____

_____

_____

_____

_____

_____

_____

_____

_____

_____

_____

_____

_____

_____

_____

_____

_____

_____

Now here's the follow-up question I want us to think through: *How have I become who I am?*

We'll explore this question in the pages ahead, but let me give you the bottom line. The answer not only tells you how you have become who you are, but *how you are becoming who you will be.* Here it is:

## You are being molded.

The apostle Paul writes in Romans 12:2, "Do not conform to the pattern of this world, but be transformed by the renewing of your mind." The original Greek word Paul uses, which is translated "conform," is *suschematizo.* (Pronunciation: Take the tip of your pointer finger and connect it to the tip of your thumb, forming a circle. Now try saying that word with an Italian accent.) *Suschematizo* means to be molded by something external. *The New Testament in Modern English* reads, "Don't let the world around you squeeze you into its own mould, but let God re-mould your minds from within" (PHILLIPS).

Paul starts with "do not," which in the Greek is written in the present imperative verb tense, to convey "stop doing this." The command implies the believers in Rome were already allowing themselves to be shaped by the pattern of the world.

I am spending this year going through the book of Romans with our church. In preparation I spent some time in the city of Rome. I would describe ancient Rome as a "mold machine." Rome brought people from many different cultures and backgrounds with the intention of molding them so they'd all become more *Roman.* Rome seemed to know something Paul alludes to in Romans 12—*conforming happens.* If you can influence the way people think about things, they will be conformed, whether they want to be or not.

That was true then, and it is true now.

I am not a culture basher. I watch TV and movies, know the moves to the cupid shuffle, and may have even seen a TikTok video or two, but I'm convinced we need to understand that the world has certain patterns.

And it is constantly trying to squeeze us into its mold. As you think about how your life has been molded, you may find yourself becoming defensive:

**I didn't know.
It wasn't intentional.
It was just a mold.**

That may be true, but whether or not it was intentional, our lives always come out in the shape they are molded in. To a great extent, this mold is determined by our thoughts. Proverbs 4:23 (GNT) puts it this way: "Be careful how you think; your life is shaped by your thoughts." Neuroscience is finally catching up with the wisdom of Scripture, and we are discovering just how true that is.

Dr. Caroline Leaf is a communication pathologist, audiologist, and clinical and research neuroscientist who specializes in psychoneurobiology and metacognitive neuropsychology. In other words, she's an expert in the science of how our lives are shaped by our thoughts. She contends that the average person may have more than thirty thousand thoughts per day. Of those, so many are negative, she posits, that the vast majority of the illnesses that plague us today are a direct result of a toxic thought life.[2] And not only that. Most of these thoughts can be repetitive, which implies that the most likely scenario is that we will continue to think the thoughts we have been thinking. These thought patterns eventually form a mold that shapes much of who we are.

Let's identify some ways our thoughts mold our lives, and along the way, I'll ask you some questions to help you think about your own "thought mold."

### Our Thoughts Establish Our Emotions

It can often seem as though our emotions are outside of our control, and therefore we can't help the way we feel. Or we assume we would feel differently if our circumstances were different. But there is an intricate relationship between our thoughts and our feelings. God created our brains with a limbic system, specifically the amygdala, which helps us process our emotional and behavioral responses. These responses are intimately connected to our ability to survive. If you've ever felt that immediate response in a situation of sudden fear or danger, that's your limbic system kicking into gear. It's very powerful, even shaping our memories to help us understand and avoid danger.

But we're not at its mercy. The prefrontal cortex, which is where we do our intentional, high-level thinking, can modulate the amygdala's response. MRI scans have demonstrated that when participants reframe negative images using intentional thinking, there is a reduction in negative and unwanted emotions. What does that mean? *God has given us the tools to help shape our behavior.* This is an incredible gift of freedom. We are not just bundles of reactions in a mechanistic world. We have agency, dignity, and choice.

Here's what this looks like. Stephanie feels intense anxiety before a job interview. Her heart begins racing (amygdala response). But then, by intentionally reminding herself of her qualifications and thinking about past successes, she reduces her anxiety and feels more confident (prefrontal cortex modulating the amygdala). As a result, she presents as calmer and more competent in a business setting and performs better in the interview.

Mark feels frustrated and angry when stuck in traffic and late for a dinner date. He begins gripping the steering wheel tightly (amygdala response). But then, by realizing what he's doing and consciously deciding to view this as an opportunity to listen to an audiobook, he feels calmer and even a bit positive about the delay (prefrontal cortex intervention). He shows up to the meal ready to enjoy the time, despite the additional twenty minutes on the freeway.

Our neurotransmitter system also connects our thoughts with our emotions. What we think about can trigger the release of neurotransmitters like serotonin, dopamine, and norepinephrine, all of which can influence our emotional state.

Here's how that connection might play out: Emily thinks about her upcoming vacation to Hawaii. Neurotransmitter effect: This triggers the release of dopamine, the "reward" neurotransmitter. Emotional result: Emily feels excited and motivated, looking forward to her trip.

Alex spends a few minutes each morning thinking about the things he's grateful for. Neurotransmitter effect: This practice increases serotonin levels, often associated with mood regulation. Emotional result: Alex experiences an improved mood and a greater sense of contentment throughout the day.

This is the way God has made us, and when we understand it, we can begin to take a more intentional role in experiencing the emotions of life. (It will also help us appreciate the Bible's encouragement to set our minds on things above and similar statements. *Oh, yeah. God knows how our brains work.*)

Here are some questions to think about as you process the connection between your mind and your emotions:

- What situation consistently triggers a strong emotional response in me?
- What is the situation, and what is the response?
- How do my emotions shift when I intentionally change my thinking?

## Our Thoughts Direct Our Decisions

Have you ever made a decision and then tried to understand what led you to make it? It turns out that just like our emotions, our decisions are largely determined by what's happening in the prefrontal cortex. In fact, this part of the brain is often referred to as the executive center because that's where decisions get made. Our thoughts assign benefits and consequences to different actions based on what we think about, what we have experienced, and what we think about what we have experienced. The more we become aware of our own thought patterns, the more deliberate and objective we can be in making decisions.

Psychologist Jonathan Haidt tells the story of the elephant and the rider to help us understand the connection between our thoughts and actions.[3] He asks us to imagine a rider on top of an elephant. Think of the rider as our conscious rational mind, while the elephant in this case represents our subconscious or automatic decisions. The rider may think they are in charge, and the elephant may go along with their direction, but in reality, the elephant has the power to go in any direction it wants—and there is nothing the rider can do about it. At least in the moment. But what if that rider had spent time and care to *train* the elephant? Perhaps once in a while, there would still be a problem—that's only natural—but the situation would be totally different from that of the untrained elephant.

We like to think we can be in charge of our own direction and decisions in any given moment, but in reality, the thoughts we have been thinking have established neural pathways that will decide which direction we go. This is why we can all think of decisions we've made that don't align with what we say we want. Our established thought patterns are guiding our behavior in ways we underestimate. The way we change our decision-making patterns is to take the time to train the elephant by changing our thinking and redirecting our neural pathways.

You commit to eating healthier and plan to have a salad for lunch, but when lunchtime comes, you find yourself hungry for the fast food you've been eating for the past several months.

You set your alarm for 6:00 a.m. to spend time reading the Bible and praying before you start your day, but when the alarm goes off, your body reaches for the snooze button without a second thought.

You decide to have a calm and rational discussion with your wife about finances, but during the conversation, your emotions take over. You start raising your voice and being defensive.

In all these examples, your established thought pattern is making the decision for you. Lasting change requires more than behavior modification; it requires intentional and consistent thought transformation.

The challenge is that we've been thinking the way we've been thinking for a long time, and our thinking becomes ingrained. If you think about it, the easiest thoughts to think are the thoughts you've already been thinking. But for things to change, you have to change your thinking. That's a lot to think about.

This is why we so often *don't* change.

We assume the path to transformation is behavior modification, so we set a New Year's resolution or make a vow to quit a bad habit. We swear, "We really mean it this time!" and then . . . we go back to doing the same old thing, all over again.

Why? You really meant it when you said you were going to change, so why didn't you? Because you focused on changing your behavior but not your thinking. And what you do is primarily determined not by your intentions but by your thoughts.

Here are some questions to think about as you process the connection between your thoughts and your decisions:

- What habits am I trying to break but keep falling back into?
- When do I find myself saying, *I don't know why I did that?*
- In what areas of my life is there a disconnect between what I do and what I want to do?
- What strategies have I implemented to try to make changes?

### Our Thoughts Regulate Our Relationships

Cognitive interpretation is how your mind explains events and situations—everything from what pops up in your news feed to the passing comment of a coworker. How we think about others' words and actions directly influences how we treat and emotionally respond to them. If we allow our thoughts to habitually be negative, even when the person's behavior or words are ambiguous, we will often react in a way that is defensive or overly sensitive and puts a strain on the relationship.

Can you see how cognitive interpretation largely determines how we treat the people around us? Our thoughts provide a filter that interprets what people say and do, which in turn determines our emotional response and personal connection.

When I was struggling with some of my relationships at work, a friend challenged me. He explained that my mind was "filling in the gaps" with negative assumptions and critical explanations. In all of our relationships, we have certain gaps to fill. Sometimes it's an information gap, where we don't have all the information we need to make a certain decision. It could be a context gap, where we don't understand the context in which a certain comment was made. Other times, it's a connection gap, where our lives have gotten so busy that we haven't spent time together.

With our thoughts we are constantly filling in gaps, and we have to decide if we are going to presume the worst or assume the best. Are we going to give a cynical or a generous explanation? Are we going to think positive or negative thoughts? The point is that when we fill in the gaps, how we think will significantly impact our relationships.

When I pull in the driveway and see that my wife has ordered another item on Amazon that has been delivered to the house but I don't know what's in the box, my next thoughts will fill in the gap. I can think to myself, *How can we possibly need something else? We've had deliveries every day this week. Doesn't she care how much money we're spending?* Or I can think a different thought: *I never have to wonder if we are going to have what we need in our house. My wife is thoughtful to take care of everything, and no one loves a good deal more than she does.*

What I think in that moment has the power to regulate my relationship with my spouse and determine the course of our connection for the rest of the evening. It is also likely to be more accurate to the situation, as we are able to adopt a more rational perspective that can help make sense of the whole context and all pertinent information, not just your emotive response.

Here are some questions to think about as you process this connection between your thoughts and your relationships:

- When I make assumptions about someone's intentions, do I assume the best, or do I assume the worst?
- When I think about my past with this person, what do I remember?

- What narrative do I tell myself about this person when I have to fill in the gaps?

## Our Thoughts Guide Our Goals

Our thoughts about our possibilities can determine the goals we set and the purposes we pursue in our lives. When our thoughts align with our desired goals, we are much more likely to take the appropriate action.

Think of one or two goals you have for yourself right now. If you take time to think about how accomplishing them can have a positive impact on your life, it triggers the neurotransmitter dopamine. Dopamine neurons respond not only to experiencing rewards but to thinking about rewards. So by thinking about our goals, we are more motivated to pursue them. The more we think about our goals, the more aware we become of our current state vis-à-vis our desired outcome.

This is why a prime advertising strategy for diet and exercise programs is to show before and after pictures. They want you to think about your current state and focus on a desired outcome. The more you think about the desired outcome, the more motivated you will be to live in a way that aligns with that goal.

James Nesmeth, a United States Air Force pilot, was held as a prisoner of war in Vietnam for seven years. He was an average golfer before he was captured, usually shooting in the mid-90s, which I would be thrilled with. But during his seven-year imprisonment, when he was often in solitary confinement, he passed the time and maintained his sanity by visualizing himself playing at his favorite golf course. Nearly every day for those seven years, Nesmeth would play in his mind a full eighteen holes on that course he knew so well. He would think through the details—the clubs he would use, the smell of the grass, and the flight of the ball. Sometimes he would spend four hours thinking about playing those eighteen holes.

When he was finally released, he returned home and went to that golf course. Despite not having played golf for seven years, he shot a 74, better than his best score before he was captured.[4]

The thoughts we think are always taking us somewhere. They can get us closer to our goals, or they can move us in the opposite direction. Paul understood the power of this dynamic when he wrote in Philippians 3 that he was intentionally *not* thinking about what was in his past but instead thinking about what lies ahead.

Here are some questions to think about as you process this connection between your thoughts and your goals:

- What are my most important goals right now?
- How often do I think about them?
- When I think about these goals, do I focus more on the obstacles or on the desired outcome?
- Do I pray about my goals to make sure my thoughts are aligned with what God wants for my life?

## TRANSFORMED

If your life is shaped by your thoughts, what mold are you being squeezed into? In Romans 12:2, Paul tells us not to be conformed and then juxtaposes that with an alternative: "but be transformed by the renewal of your mind."

We like to think we are nonconformists. *You are not the boss of me. No one tells me what to do. I'm living my own truth.* But everyone conforms to something. When Paul tells us not to be conformed but rather to be transformed, he is implying that it will be one or the other.

Choice A: Conform to this world.

Choice B: Be transformed by God into the image of Jesus so you can live out God's "good, pleasing and perfect will" (Romans 12:2).

Choice C: There is no option C.

*Transformed* is the English word that translates the *metamorphoo*, a word that may seem familiar, because it's where we get *metamorphosis*. Remember in elementary school when you learned about how a caterpillar becomes a butterfly, transforming from something kind of icky that crawls around in the mud into something beautiful that soars through the sky? That's a picture of God's goal for you. Instead of being molded by something external, we can be transformed by God from the inside out.

God intends for your life to be beautiful. You are God's workmanship, his poetry (see Ephesians 2:10). He has something amazing in mind for your life, but if it is to become reality, you need to be transformed to become who God desires you to become. What could be better than that?

*You should do this for you* so you can become the person you want to see in the mirror someday, the best version of you for the people you care about, but there's another reason, and, honestly, it's even better. *You should do this for God.*

Romans 12:1 says that the motivation to be transformed by the renewing of our minds is God's mercy and grace toward us. That verse begins, "In view of God's mercy." Often our motives for self-improvement revolve around ourselves, and while this reason for transformation will help us, it's not the primary why. Instead, we want to be transformed because of God's love so we live in a way that may be opposite and offensive to the world around us but will be holy and pleasing to him.

It's also important to note that "be transformed" uses the passive imperative tense. The word *passive* means we are not the ones who do it; it is done *to us.* God is the only one who can do this, and he wants to do it in you and me. We will talk at length about taking our thoughts captive and renewing our minds, but let me be clear from the beginning that this is not a self-help approach to transformation. It is a spiritual journey empowered by the Holy Spirit. As we renew our minds, God is the one who brings about the transformation.

The word *imperative* shows that it is a command, which is interesting because, again, it's not something we can do. Remember, this action is expressed in the passive tense; it's done to us. Typically, we're not commanded to do things we can't do, but here we have a different story. Why? We have a part to play, a choice to make. Transformation is not something God will do in us against our will. Taking every thought captive means submitting every thought to him. As we learn to do that, he will bring about transformation.

Being transformed by the renewing of our minds is not something that happens automatically or accidently; it takes intentionality and effort. This is not a stroll in the park; it's a tug-of-war. Our spiritual formation is *counter*transformation. We battle against our flesh, our old sinful habits, the world we live in, our enemy who rules over it, and the mold that always seems to be squeezing us.* If we don't choose transformation, we won't just sit in neutral; we will be left to the persistent molding of the world, dragged in the opposite direction of who we wanted to become.

If we are transformed by the renewing of our minds, the real transformation question is this: *How do we renew our minds?* Here's the answer: We learn to take every thought captive.

---

* The Bible says that Satan is "the god of this world" (2 Corinthians 4:4 NLT; see also John 12:31; Ephesians 2:2; Colossians 1:13).

## CHAPTER 2

# THE LAW OF COGNITION

## HOW THOUGHTS BECOME LIFE

After doing some research, I've concluded that there aren't a lot of "gravity deniers" out there. But let's imagine a man named Jack, who, well, doesn't believe in gravity. He's always been a bit of a contrarian who wondered whether gravity is a hoax perpetuated by the scientific community. The more he thought about it, the more convinced he became. He would argue, "It's all about density and buoyancy, not some invisible force." Some of his friends and family tried to reason with him; in a spirit of acceptance, others told him he could think whatever he wanted to about gravity. The problem is, the more Jack thought about it, the more convinced he became that gravity wasn't real.

One day, Jack decided to prove his point once and for all. He announced he would jump from the roof of his two-story house, confident he would float instead of fall. Horrified onlookers watched as he leaped off the edge of the roof.

Gravity didn't care what Jack thought.

Gravity acted the way it always acts.

Jack ended up with multiple fractures and a severe concussion. He spent the next number of weeks in the hospital rethinking his thoughts on the law of gravity.

Stepping back from this imagined scenario, let's think for a moment about *our* thinking. In psychology there's a principle called "the law of cognition." Simply stated, what you think about determines who you become. More specifically, what you think about determines what you believe; what you believe determines how you feel; how you feel determines what you do and how you live. Let's say that in reverse so we don't miss the significance: What I do is determined by how I feel; how I feel is determined by what I believe; what I believe is determined by what I think about. So the question is, "What do I think about?" Because what I think about matters, even if I don't think it matters.

The law of cognition is a bit like the law of gravity. Every day, our lives are impacted and shaped by this law, even though we cannot see it. Like the law of gravity, the law of cognition doesn't require us to believe in it for it to be true. We can tell ourselves that our thinking doesn't have a significant impact on our lives, but that will turn out about as well for us as things turned out for Jack.

It turns out that this insight isn't just something from psychologists either; it's ancient wisdom. The Bible warns in Proverbs 4:23 (GNT), "Be careful how you think; your life is shaped by your thoughts." Either you take your thoughts captive, or they will take you captive.

A number of years ago, I sat down with a group of men, and we spent a few hours talking about the thoughts we had as boys that have held us captive as men. Here are a few things that were shared:

*I didn't think it was okay to be sad.* Joe grew up in a home where the expectation was to be happy. All the time. No matter what. Joe's dad set the example. Real men might get angry, but they were never sad. Being sad is for weak people. When the family dog died, Joe and his sisters cried, and his dad laughed at him for crying. Now as a man, he struggles with loneliness because when he's sad, he's ashamed to share it. He also deals with anger issues because it's not okay get sad, but it's okay to be angry.

*I thought of women as objects.* Mike's parents divorced when he was six. When he would stay at his father's house, he had easy access to his dad's collection of porn magazines. When he turned sixteen, his dad hired an escort for him so he would "know what he was doing." By the time he got married, he had slept with so many women that he couldn't even remember all their names. In the early years of his marriage, he was demanding when it came to their sex life and put unhealthy pressure on his wife. They were constantly fighting about sex and got divorced after three years.

*I thought my worth was determined by how much money I made.* Dave grew up thinking success in life was determined by the job he had, the car he drove, and the house he lived in. He was surrounded by examples that reinforced his thinking that the measure of his worth was his net worth. Those thoughts have directed every major decision in his life. He discovered he was aiming at a moving target. No matter how much he had it was never enough.

*I thought I couldn't ask for help.* That one was mine. I grew up in a home with a mother who was a counselor and a father who was a college president. They both excel in helping other people, and somewhere along the line, I started to think, *It's okay to help people, but it's not okay to need help from people.* I thought that asking for help was admitting failure, that I was always supposed to be a rescuer, not someone who would ever need to be rescued. Those thoughts didn't seem to be a problem. At least until I needed help.

In the early years of marriage when my wife and I were struggling, I was surrounded by people who could have helped us and a young wife who desperately wanted me to ask for support. But I refused. When we were in the thick of parenting and struggling with one of our children, I had people all around me who could have given me counsel, but I wouldn't ask for it. The thought, *I can't ask for help*, wasn't just holding *me* captive; it was holding my wife and kids captive as well.

## STRONGHOLDS

*Stronghold* is a scriptural word that describes the areas of our lives where our thoughts have taken us captive. A stronghold is a lie we believe and live by. Strongholds are formed by ingrained patterns of thinking that are opposed to God's truth and wisdom. Thoughts become beliefs, beliefs become actions, and actions determine our lives, so we had better be sure our thoughts are true.

In ancient times, a stronghold was a building, a fortress built on top of the highest peak in a city or in a place that was most defendable against attack. This building had reinforced walls all around as high as twenty feet. In times when the city was under attack, the stronghold was thought to be the one place that was impenetrable, the place where those in power would hide so they wouldn't be captured or killed.

In the Bible, a comparison is made between these strongholds and the thoughts we think that are counter to the truth of God. Lies that have been reinforced so many times, lies we keep so protected that they're almost impenetrable. We have *mental* strongholds. And until we take them captive, they will hold *us* captive.

Throughout this book, you will read several short parables to help you think through certain concepts related to our mental strongholds. Jesus often taught by stories, in part to encourage his audience to pause and think about what he was teaching rather than simply take in information. We've become so adept at consuming content, but a real *story* can help us slow down and process. I've wrapped the idea of strongholds in story form to help us better understand the concept of strongholds in Scripture:*

---

\* I'm not the first to do this, by the way. The Puritan writer John Bunyan, most famous for *Pilgrim's Progress*, wrote a book called *The Holy War* in which the city of Mansoul is the center of a war between God, who was working to recapture it, and the devil, who made it his stronghold.

## A PARABLE: THE BATTLE FOR MENTIS

In the rolling hills of a distant land stood a great city called Mentis. This city was unlike any other, for it existed within the mind of every person. At the center of Mentis, atop the highest hill, loomed an imposing fortress known as the Stronghold of Lies.

For generations, the people of Mentis lived in the shadow of this stronghold. It had been there for so long that people had forgotten it had not been there forever. Its walls were built from vast stones of false beliefs, cemented together through years of reinforced patterns of thinking. The fortress was guarded by Fear and Pride, who turned away any who dared to question its authority.

One day, a humble messenger named Truth arrived at the gates of Mentis. He carried with him scrolls of wisdom from the Great King who ruled over all cities of the mind. Truth called out to the people, "The King sends word that you need not live under the tyranny of the stronghold. He offers you freedom and a new way of thinking."

Many of the citizens, however, were too afraid to listen. They had lived so long under the stronghold's influence that its lies felt like safety. Who else would protect them? Some even attacked Truth, driven by Fear and Pride.

But there was one young woman named Hope, who heard Truth's words and felt a stirring in her heart. Despite the warnings of her fellow citizens, she approached Truth and read the scrolls he carried.

As Hope read, she felt as though the scales were falling from her eyes. She saw the stronghold for what it truly was—a prison of deception. With newfound courage, she decided to help Truth spread the King's message.

Together, Truth and Hope began to chip away at the foundations of the stronghold. It was hard work, and they often felt overwhelmed by the task. The stronghold had stood for so long that many believed it to be indestructible.

Slowly but surely, more citizens joined their cause. Love brought his warmth to melt the cold hearts turned hard by lies. Faith provided the strength to persevere when the task seemed impossible. Grace offered forgiveness to those who had long defended the stronghold.

As more people accepted Truth, bricks began to fall from the stronghold's walls. Fear and Pride found themselves outnumbered by a growing army of believers armed with the King's wisdom.

Finally, after much struggle and perseverance, the last wall of the stronghold crumbled. In its place, the citizens began to build a new structure—the Temple of Truth. Unlike the old fortress that cast shadows over the city, this new building shone with light, illuminating every corner of Mentis.

With Truth's help the people learned to guard their minds against new lies that might try to rebuild that old fortress.

And so the city of Mentis was transformed. The message of freedom spread to other cities, and a great revolution of truth soon swept across the land of minds, one liberated thought at a time.

## EMPOWERED LIES

A helpful way to identify a stronghold in your life is to think about an area in which you feel stuck. You're not sure *why* you're stuck; you just know you're stuck. As you think about that area, ask yourself, *Is there a lie I'm believing?*

When you believe a lie, you give it the power of truth in your life.

As you were growing up, did your parents tell you it was harmful to crack your knuckles? Maybe they even made a rule that you couldn't do it? It's a great rule. The only problem is, it's not true. It's *not* particularly problematic to crack your knuckles. You won't get arthritis. Nor will you end up with deformed fingers that will keep anyone from wanting to marry you.

It's just not true.

One of the ways we know it's false is that there is a California doctor who did an experiment in which he consistently cracked the knuckles of . . . only one of his hands. After *decades* of this peculiar behavior, he did

X-rays and found no difference between his hands.[1] Another experiment with a bigger sample size came to a similar conclusion.[2]

The idea that knuckle cracking is dangerous is not true, but if we hear the wrong thing often enough, it gets into us. It becomes ingrained in our thinking, and we give it the power of truth. As we do, it shapes our behavior. The ripple effects go out from there.

Because you think, *It's dangerous to crack your knuckles*, you may have tried really hard not to do it and even told your kids they shouldn't do it either. Perhaps it prompted annoyance or arguments at some point and maybe even affected your relationships. Your thinking translates into real-life decisions that impact the people around you and teach them to think the same way you do.

The point here isn't to try to get you to crack your knuckles now, but it's simply to highlight how little lies can make little changes in our lives. And if that's true, wouldn't big lies make big changes?

When you believe a lie, you give it the power of truth in your life. The way you think determines how you live. Generational strongholds pass down broken thinking from one generation to the next.

I'm going to give you three minutes to consider some of the thoughts that have been passed down and affected your life.

To be transformed we need to renew our minds. We need to expose the lies we believe, capture those thoughts, and replace them with God's truth that can set us free.

When our thoughts become ingrained, we become attached to our lies—sometimes because we've believed them for so long and sometimes because they allow us to feel in control; sometimes because admitting something is a lie calls everything else into question and sometimes we're so used to believing them that it's more comfortable to just keep believing them. And sometimes it's because so many of the people around us and so much of the information we are exposed to support the lie that we don't question it.

## HOW STRONGHOLDS ARE BUILT

Unlike real-life fortresses, strongholds aren't usually established intentionally. No one takes out a set of blueprints for a stronghold in their lives and gets to work. Instead, they are built in our minds by means of thoughts that haven't been taken captive.

- **Early and frequent thinking:** A more technical term is cognitive schema development, which teaches that the mental framework we develop to filter information and determine our responses, even as adults, is shaped by our early input and experiences.[3] The thought patterns we were exposed to at a young age can create strongholds we never wanted and didn't intentionally choose.

  Talk to someone who grew up in a home where there was a lot of yelling and screaming. They will tell you they promised themselves it was going to be different for them, but they all too often deal with conflict in the same way, or they totally withdraw, which can be just as detrimental. Because the brain is most plastic in early childhood, it's often a time when strongholds are built without our realization.

- **Repeated thoughts:** We will talk more about neural pathways later, but for now it's important to note that our thoughts are not just abstract concepts, but they actually contribute to our brain's structure. We can actively choose to shape our neural pathways or passively allow neural pathways to form. Many of our strongholds come from neural pathways that have been formed over time, often handed down to us, intentionally or not.

- **Emotional association:** Thoughts connected to strong emotions have a way of forming lasting patterns. This is why one of my closest friends had to work through strongholds established when his dad died when he was in elementary school. Those emotions created thoughts in him at a young age that went something like this: *No one understands what I'm going through, so I should keep it to myself,* and *I need to be perfect so no one else will leave me.* Strongholds built by loneliness and fear are hard to tear down.

- **Cognitive reinforcement:** This building block refers to our instinct to surround ourselves with voices and opinions that will reinforce what we already think. We search for information and interpretation that will affirm our thoughts rather than challenge them. This is also referred to as confirmation bias.

Avery's parents got divorced when she was ten because her dad cheated on her mom and ran off with another woman. The thought that *all men cheat* was planted in her, and she began to give selective attention to other examples of men cheating. Avery married a man named Steve, and about a year into their marriage, Steve came home from work and mentioned a new female coworker. Avery became upset and started to look through his phone and make accusations. Steve felt distrusted and started to withdraw emotionally, which Avery saw as further evidence. Avery has a stronghold of distrust that has been built by her thoughts around a hurt she experienced. She interprets new experiences by looking for evidence that supports that thought. Unless that stronghold gets torn down, it will tear apart her relationship.

## HOW STRONGHOLDS ARE DESTROYED

Proverbs 21:22 provides practical advice for those who find themselves having to attack a city: "One who is wise can go up against the city of the mighty and pull down the stronghold in which they trust." The idea is this: If you're attacking a city, you better make sure you get the stronghold. If you attack the city but *don't* take the more difficult action of bringing down the stronghold, the city will reestablish itself because its leaders are hiding in the stronghold. So whatever else you do, make sure you bring down the stronghold.

The stronghold must fall.

The same is true for us. If we want to change our lives, to become the person we are meant to be, it's not enough to change our behavior and address our habits. The behavior will come back later and old habits will return, often stronger than before. Or we'll replace one thing with something similar—one self-destructive habit gets swapped out for another, because the stronghold is still standing.

How do we bring down a stronghold? By taking our thoughts captive. By grabbing hold of every thought and submitting it to the light of truth.

Let's take another look at 2 Corinthians 10:3–5. This time take note of what we're supposed to demolish and the power we're to use to make that happen.

> For though we live in the world, we do not wage war as the world does. The weapons we fight with are not the weapons of the world. On the contrary, they have divine power to demolish strongholds. We demolish arguments and every pretension that sets itself up against the knowledge of God, and we take captive every thought to make it obedient to Christ.
>
> 2 CORINTHIANS 10:3–5

Paul writes that we need to "demolish strongholds." He then restates it as "demolish arguments and every pretension that sets itself up against the knowledge of God." These are all things that happen on the battlefield of our minds. Human reasoning and arguments that oppose the truth of God are thoughts that need to be taken captive and destroyed.

We can't be passive about this. We don't wait and hope things get better. We can take out the rest of the city, but if we don't take down the stronghold, nothing is going to change. This is why we end up making the same resolutions year after year. This is why we feel frustrated with our progress and don't understand how, despite our best effort and genuine intentions, we are still fighting the same battles years, even decades, later.

In our minds is a ring where we have competing thoughts that are wrestling with each other.

Let's play this idea out, and I acknowledge this will be a little cheesy, but I want us to get a mental picture of how our stronghold thoughts must be challenged and submitted. Imagine this scene unfolding in your mind. In a dimly lit arena, two thoughts circle each other. One is a seasoned veteran we'll call *Worry*. A mass of tangled nerves and frantic energy, this thought holds the title belt and has for a long time. The challenger is the underdog we'll call *Trust*. This thought is new to The Octagon but stands tall with quiet confidence.

The bell rings.

Worry charges forward, throwing a wild haymaker of worst-case scenarios. "Everything is falling apart," it shouts in a voice filled with panic.

Trust sidesteps gracefully. "God is in control," it counters in a steady and reassuring tone.

Undeterred, Worry launches into a frenzy of "what ifs." "You can't control anything!" it shrieks, attempting to grapple Trust into submission.

But Trust stands firm, its foundation unshaken. It absorbs the blows and retaliates with a powerful jab of perspective based in Scripture: "Nothing can separate me from the love of God," a powerful thought that lands squarely on Worry's chin.

Worry stumbles, momentarily disoriented. Trust seizes the opportunity, moving in with a combination of deep breaths and biblical thinking. "I can cast all my worries on God because he cares for me."

Worry tries a counterattack but can't find its footing. Trust presses in with thoughts of faith and hope.

Gasping for air, Worry taps out.

Trust has won this fight, but Worry knows in the octagon of the mind, a rematch will soon come.

I told you it would be cheesy, but it makes the point. The thoughts that have built strongholds in your life must be challenged and subdued with thoughts rooted in God's power and promises. They won't give up without a fight. So we'll have to take that fight to them, with God's help.

## I CAN'T. HE CAN.

All of this sounds good. But just as not all of us can step into a fight with a seasoned opponent and be confident we will win, not all of us can press in like this in our own power. In fact, I'll bet *none* of us can. I've tried, and I know I can't. So let's think about power for a minute.

More than a decade ago, my wife talked me into moving onto a farm. She grew up as a farmer's daughter who knew her way around tools and tractors. I did not. I grew up in a neighborhood, where my dad had a hammer and a few screwdrivers he kept in a drawer but never used. When we moved onto the farm, I wanted to cut some trails through the woods where my wife and daughters could ride horses. Trees would need to be removed and branches cut down. I got on my ATV with an axe I bought from Lowe's and attempted to cut down the first of dozens of trees that had to be removed. A few hours later, the tree was still standing, but I was about ready to fall over. I went back to Lowe's and bought a chainsaw. I had never used one before and wasn't very confident. I bought one of the smallest and cheapest ones—small enough that if things went wrong, it might cause a flesh wound but wouldn't cost me a limb. I got it home and powered it up, but within minutes, the chain was stuck in the tree. I needed something bigger.

We have a store close to where I live called Chainsaw World. I had never been in that store and immediately felt out of place upon entering.

But I was desperate. I told the guy working that I was cutting some trails and felling some trees. He told me I needed a chainsaw called Farm Boss. I questioned whether I needed something with that much power. He looked at me and said, "The Farm Boss needs a Farm Boss."

Truthfully, my wife is 100 percent The Farm Boss; I'm the farmhand. But he didn't need to know that. The price was steep, just under five hundred dollars. I knew the real farm boss would not approve. The salesman put it in my hands and told me it would cut through those trees like butter.

I took it home and got to work on those trails and couldn't believe the difference. Turns out, I just needed a tool strong and powerful enough to do the work to clear the trails.

When we are taking down the strongholds in our minds, we are trying to clear the path for some new trails. We need some new neural pathways, and having the right kind of power is essential. We don't use the tools of the world; 2 Corinthians 10:4 says we have "divine power" to take down these strongholds.

It's with God's power that you will "take captive every thought to make it obedient to Christ" (2 Corinthians 10:5). Every time you have one of those old thoughts, those strongly held lies, you will identify it and cut it down. You won't just accept it because it fits into your mind or because you've thought it so many times before. You won't just go with it because it's reinforced by the people around you. No, you will take it captive and submit it to the truth of Jesus. *That's* how you defeat strongholds.

You recognize the lie and call it out as a lie, and then you replace it with truth. As you do, your thinking will begin to change. As your thinking changes, so will your behavior. You will begin to experience true transformation.

That's the plan, but, again, we're not capable of doing it in our own power. The first thought you may need to rethink is the thought that you can do this on your own. If those tools would work, they would've worked by now. We've tried self-empowerment and self-motivation and self-help plans, and they don't work. Today, we declare freedom, our emancipation, from relying on our power. We are transitioning to divine power.

So we need to fight. We need the power to fight. Got it. That sounds nice. But *how*?

How do we access God's power to tear down the strongholds? How do we step into the ring and get rough with the thoughts that are getting rough with us? How do we get our hands on some different tools? That's what we'll discover in the next section of the book—how to access God's "Farm Boss" power so we can demolish strongholds, taking our lies captive and replacing them with truth so that our minds are renewed. Then, instead of being conformed to culture, we will be transformed by God into the people we are meant to be.

And it all happens in our minds.

## CHAPTER 3

# THE RULE OF EXPOSURE

## THE HIDDEN INFLUENCE OF INPUT

H e was rejected *eight hundred* times.

Can you imagine?

Seth Godin was twenty-four years old, wrote a book, sent it to publishers, and according to him, received eight hundred rejection letters in that first year. Every door he knocked on was slammed in his face.

If that was you, what would happen in your thought life? There would be an overwhelming temptation to go dark and negative—to think you're a failure, to feel like it's impossible, that it's never going to happen. Who wouldn't feel that way?

With each rejection, I expect Godin's mind would have been filled with discouragement and doubt. My guess is that after the first four hundred or so rejections, he would have had thoughts of resentment and frustration. Left unchecked, his mind almost certainly would have been filled with thoughts of giving up, not just on that book, but on writing all together.

Now I'm not saying we're all going to be Seth Godin, who of course went on to be a bestselling author. We can't always control outcomes, but we *can* control where we're setting our thoughts. And to do that has a lot more power than we think. Will a sharpshooter always hit their target? Of course not. *But that doesn't mean they don't carefully take aim.*

All things being equal, we will tend to become what we think. Our thoughts will determine which direction we go.

Back that up and think it through: *I can change the direction of my life by changing what I think about. So, then, what determines what I think about?*

But back to Seth Godin, who wanted to answer this question, and so he turned to . . . Zig Ziglar—a Christian and a motivational speaker committed to thinking positively and inspiring people to believe in their work. Seth explains how he got through all the rejections without quitting, with a *major* dose of Zig, delivered via motivational tapes: "It wasn't self-talk, it was Zig-talk. Zig Ziglar talked to me every day for three hours. For three hours a day, for three years, I listened to this guy. . . . I knew it by heart because there were only seventy-two hours' worth of stuff. That voice in my head took over because I didn't have the voice I needed in my head."[1]

Godin listened to his library of seventy-two hours of Zig Ziglar recordings—three hours a day, every day, for *three years*. That's 3,285 hours of taking in intentional thoughts. It's like pouring fresh, clear water into a stagnant pond. At first, you might not notice much change, but if you keep adding gallons and gallons of clean water, the murky water is gradually replaced.

Godin's negative thoughts didn't stand a chance. He says, "The only thing that kept me from quitting and getting a job as a bank teller were the tapes that Zig did."[2] By the way, it's a good thing Godin didn't quit. He has since written twenty-two bestselling books in thirty-nine languages.[3]

I'm not sure if Godin knew what he was doing, but by listening to 3,285 hours of lectures on repeat he was leveraging what we'll call "the rule of exposure." The rule of exposure has a symbiotic connection with the law of cognition. The law of cognition emphasizes that our thoughts determine who we are, and the rule of exposure says that our thoughts will tend to match whatever we're exposed to the most.

So to sum up:

- What we are exposed to determines our thoughts.
- Our thoughts determine our beliefs.
- Our beliefs determine our behaviors.
- Our behaviors shape our lives.

This isn't just me saying this, by the way. The rule of exposure is rooted in a psychological phenomenon first identified by Robert Zajonc in 1968 that he called "the mere exposure effect."[4] It refers to our tendency to prefer or be drawn to ideas or individuals we have the most common and repeated exposure to. What we are most exposed to shapes our thoughts and beliefs, which in turn directs our lives. One of the dynamics of this effect is that the exposure doesn't even have to be conscious or intentional for the effect to be realized. Subconscious and unintentional exposure will shape your thoughts and direct your life without requiring your permission.

In 2004, a study was published in *Pediatrics* magazine called "Watching Television Predicts Adolescent Initiation of Sexual Behavior."[5] Researchers surveyed more than seventeen hundred adolescents ages twelve to seventeen about their television viewing habits and sexual behavior and then followed up with these same students a year later. The students who watched more sexual content on television were demonstrably more likely to have engaged in sexual behavior. The mere repeated exposure to sexual content influenced the students' attitudes and beliefs toward sex, as well as the likelihood of engaging in sexual activity.

Consider similar studies:

- Children exposed to violent content are more likely to exhibit aggressive behavior later in life.[6]
- Subliminal exposure to brand logos influences and determines consumer purchases.[7]
- Repeated exposure to pornography shapes sexual attitudes, expectations, and practices.[8]
- Exposure to food advertisements lead people to choose and consume the advertised foods, even when not hungry.[9]

- Frequent exposure to idealized body images on social media leads to increased body dissatisfaction and eating disorders, especially among young women.[10]
- Excessive exposure to dramatic news events can lead people to anxiously overestimate the likelihood of experiencing similar events.[11]

One simple equation that can be applied to these studies supporting the mere exposure effect:

Input = Output.
Input: *the content we are repeatedly exposed to*
Output: *the thoughts we have that shape our beliefs and behaviors*

This is the way God made us. Neuroplasticity demonstrates that our brains have the ability to form synaptic connections through repeated exposure. The exposure establishes and reinforces neural pathways associated with whatever we are exposed to.

Now at this point, you may be panicking a little. You're putting the pieces together, aren't you? You see how influenced we are by things outside our control—maybe even outside of our awareness. We are shaped by our environment, by exposure to things we often don't even choose consciously. But here's the good news: You are not helpless in this process. In fact, this is where the transformative power of taking every thought captive comes into play.

God in his infinite wisdom created our brains with this amazing capacity for change. This neuroplasticity isn't a flaw or a vulnerability it's a gift. It means that no matter what patterns have been established in your mind, no matter what negative influences have shaped your thinking in the past, your Creator has created you with the ability to change.

So instead of feeling overwhelmed by the influences around you, I encourage you to see this as an opportunity. You have the power, through Christ, to shape your mind. By taking your thoughts captive, by choosing what you expose yourself to, you can partner with God in the process of your own transformation.

## EVERYTHING FLOWS

When we see the need for change in our lives, our first instinct is to focus on changing our behavior. If I see the need to lose weight, my first response isn't to think about my thoughts or the content I'm exposed to, but to go the gym and work out. But real and lasting transformation begins in our minds.

A series of tests were done to evaluate how well a person can make decisions in a crisis. In one test, a person was taken into a bathroom where a bathtub was quickly filling with water. They were told their job was to empty the tub as quickly as possible, and they were given just three items—a teaspoon, a tablespoon, and a cup.

If you were placed in this position, what would you do?

- start bailing water with the teaspoon
- start bailing water with the tablespoon
- start bailing water with the cup

It seems obvious enough, and, in fact, most people grabbed the cup and began frantically bailing water out of the tub. But a small percentage of people evaluated the situation, thought for a moment, and then turned the water off, unplugged the drain, and *then* grabbed the cup and started bailing water.

When we reach a point of crisis, when our lives are not going the way we hoped or in the direction we want, we tend to grab at what seems to be the best available option. We grab the cup and start bailing because we know *something* needs to be done. *But what if we've missed what is right in front of us? What if the first step isn't to try to change the situation but to change how we are seeing it?*

A husband finds out his wife wants to leave him because he can't control his temper. What does he do? Enroll in an anger management class.

A couple is having a hard time making the minimum payments on their credit cards. What do they do? Have a garage sale to make some quick cash.

A man starts to have chest pains. His eating and stress have caught up to him. What does he do? He goes on another diet and gets a membership at a local gym.

None of those solutions are *bad*. Quite the opposite. They are all good, and there may well be a place for them. The problem is that they focus almost exclusively on changing a behavior. *But the behavior didn't start as a behavior.* Trying to fix it isn't getting to the root of the issue.

Most of us came by this kind of strategy honestly. We've been taught to focus on our behavior our entire lives. When we were kids, we didn't get in trouble for what we *thought*; we got in trouble for what we *did*. What was rewarded or punished was our behavior. If I was disrespectful to my mom with my words, I was in trouble. But I wouldn't be punished if I just thought those things. We learned growing up that it's about behavior, and so if you want to change, change your behavior.

It is true that what we do on the outside matters, but mostly because it reveals what is on the inside. Behavior modification is like grabbing a cup and trying to get the water out of the bathtub. Yes, you will remove some of the water, but water is still flowing into the tub. So, instead, we need to figure out where the water is coming from and if there's a way to unplug the drain.

> Above all else, guard your heart,
>> for everything you do flows from it.
>
> **PROVERBS 4:23**

When Solomon, the wisest man to ever live, says "above all else," it's probably a good idea to pay attention.

There is a tendency to focus on behavior, to try to change your life by changing the way you act, but the problem is that those actions come out of your heart. So you're bailing water, but the faucet is still wide open and pouring in more water.

- You think you have a spending problem—and so you decide you're not going to spend as much, and you won't even go to the mall until you have your credit card balance paid off—but you don't have a spending problem; you have a heart problem.
- You think you have an anger problem, so you put a swear jar in the kitchen and start counting to ten, but you have a heart problem.
- You think you have an eating problem or pornography problem and so you go on a diet and install an internet filter, but what you really have is a heart problem.

You can change your behaviors, and it may help . . . a little . . . temporarily. But give it a week or a month, and you will find yourself doing the same old thing and reacting in the same old ways. Add some stress to your life, and you find yourself going down the same old path. Frustration grows as you wonder why you can never change and whether you'll ever become the person you long to be.

The problem is that the faucet is still running. Just as quickly as you're bailing out the tub, it's filling up again.

Solomon says it's about the heart. In fact, if you read through Proverbs, you'll find the word *heart* (depending on which English version you're using) right around seventy-five times. But do we know what Solomon means by heart?

It's a word we read and use a lot, but let me quote Inigo Montoya from *The Princess Bride*: "I do not think it means what you think it means." When Solomon writes about our hearts, we think we know what he means. When we hear *heart*, we think emotions, and we tend to separate the heart from the brain, where we do our thinking. Sometimes we even juxtapose our hearts and our minds. Someone might say, "You've been following your heart, but you need to think this through."

In Hebrew culture during Solomon's time, the heart and mind would have been thought of interchangeably. *Leb* is the Hebrew word translated "heart." *Leb* is a wonderful word, which refers to the inward part of us—the part that feels, desires, wills, worries, chooses, and meditates.

One definition renders it as "the inner man, mind, will, heart."[12] Did you notice it can refer to the mind *or* the heart? In fact, the same Hebrew word translated "heart" in Proverbs 4:23 is translated "mind" in 1 Samuel 9:20 (ESV, emphasis added), "As for your donkeys that were lost three days ago, do not set your *mind* on them, for they have been found." The dictionary of Old Testament words informs us this Hebrew word for *heart* "could be regarded as the seat of knowledge and wisdom," as well as "the seat of conscience and moral character."[13]

The team of scholars who translated Solomon's original Hebrew chose "guard your heart," but they could just as well have translated it "guard your mind" or "guard your thoughts."

When we ask ourselves, *Why do I keep doing this? Where is it coming from?* Solomon would say, "I know where it's coming from. It's coming from your *leb* . . . and that's why, above all else, you need to guard your *leb*."

Let me give you another word picture. Imagine you are walking in the woods and come upon a heavily polluted creek. You think, *I'm going to do something about this!* There's trash floating down the creek and lining the banks, so you start to clean it up as quickly as you can. After a few hours, you step back and see that you've made a difference. You decide to come back every day until you get all the trash removed.

The next day you go back, and . . . there is just as much trash as when you started the day before. You clean for a few hours.

The next day . . . just as much trash. Now feeling desperate, you frantically try to clear it out.

The next day . . . just as much trash.

Every day, you work until you are exhausted, and then when you return the next day, it looks like you made zero progress.

Finally, you realize you need to understand what's going on. You walk upstream to find the source of all the trash and discover that the creek runs through a garbage dump. You realize you need to change how you think about this situation. If you keep focusing on the trash in the creek, you might make a little progress, but until you address where all the garbage is coming from, you're going to keep finding yourself with the same problem.

This is why so many people find themselves living in a constant state of frustration and fatigue. Sometimes trash shows up in our lives and relationships. We don't know where it came from. We might work to get rid of it, but it keeps showing up. Why? Solomon says it's because we are allowing it to flow in. It's because we aren't guarding our *leb*. Above all else, we must guard our *leb*, because everything flows from it.

## GUARD YOUR THOUGHTS

I live in Kentucky, which is mostly known for three things starting with the letter *b*—basketball, bourbon, and bluegrass. But in Kentucky, you will also find Fort Knox, which holds about 4,600 metric tons of gold, worth around $300 billion. That's a lot of cheddar.

Fort Knox is a two-story structure reinforced with 16,500 cubic feet of granite, 1,400 tons of steel, and 4,000 cubic yards of concrete. The vault door weighs twenty tons. No one person has the combination to get in. Several staff members must each dial in separate combinations known only to them. Four guard boxes surround Fort Knox, which is also equipped with all the latest in security technology.

Why?

Because what is inside is so valuable they take every precaution to guard it. No one ever looks at all the concrete and guards and security system and thinks, *They went a little overboard.* No, what's inside is so valuable it justifies extreme measures.

Solomon implores us to go full Fort Knox on our *leb*s.

Guarding something implies there is an enemy. There is something outside trying to get inside, but you need to do whatever it takes to stop it from getting in.

That's your mind.

There are so many negative, harmful, anxious, shameful, unholy, pride-inducing, ungodly, oversexualized, hateful, helpless, selfish, jealous prompts that will pour into our minds if we let them. Sometimes they are obvious, but most of the time they try to sneak in the back door. Exposure to those things will determine our thoughts, and those thoughts will direct our lives.

## CONSTANT EXPOSURE

If our lives are shaped by our thoughts, and our thoughts reflect whatever we're exposed to the most, then what we are exposing our minds to is molding us.

When we seek change, we focus on *output*: *I need to stop doing that. I want to stop thinking that. I shouldn't talk like that anymore.*

Instead, we should focus on *input*. If we change our input, it will change our output.

You say, *I really want to be gentle*. Great. What's your input look like? If you want to be gentle but can't get enough of an angry podcaster who keeps yelling, "Everyone is against you, and it's time to fight back," then good luck with becoming gentler.

You say, *I want to be humble*. Start by checking your input. If it's constant consumerism, which always tells you to put yourself and your needs first, that you are entitled and the center of your world, it will be extremely difficult to grow in humility.

You say, *I want to be holy, to walk in purity*. What's your input? What images are you putting in your mind? Some Christians read the Bible and shake their heads in disgust at Solomon because he had a thousand wives, but they're seeking out more sexual images in a week than Solomon saw in his entire life. If that's your input, don't expect to grow in holiness.

Your input will come out in your life, one way or another.

What you are exposed to will shape your thoughts. Your thoughts will shape your life.

In John Bunyan's allegory *The Holy War*, the author pictures the heart as a city called Mansoul. In the allegory, access to Mansoul is gained through different gates. Two of the gates that have access are the Eye-gate, which is the most significant and vulnerable gate, and the Ear-gate, which is where the enemy of Mansoul first attacks the city. Bunyan explains that these gates "could never be opened nor forced, but by the will and leave of those within."[14] Whatever strategies the enemy might employ, the gates could only be opened by the people living inside. *This is bad news*, you might think.

Actually, it's *good news*. Because *you have agency*.

Let's keep going.

## THE EAR-GATE

If everything about us is being molded by our thoughts, then nothing is more important than understanding what influences the thoughts we think. We underestimate the impact of what we listen to.

When I was in high school, many churches viewed rock music as the enemy. Those were the days of Iron Maiden and Kiss. (I was more into Bon Jovi and LL Cool J.)

I remember a youth group sermon series titled *Hell's Bells*. I've since learned that this series of messages made its way through many church youth groups. We were warned that rock music would be played in hell. The message . . . kind of backfired. My friends asked, "Wait, this music is going to be in hell? I'm suddenly interested. Can you give me the names of the bands again?"

It was explained, for example, that the band name Kiss stood for "Knights in Satan's Service," and if we listened to their music, we, too, would be knights in Satan's service. They cautioned us about "back masking"—that there were hidden satanic messages in the songs if we were to play them backward. We were told if we played one particular Led Zeppelin song backward, it would say, "Here's to my sweet Satan."

The scare tactics really didn't work. That same week, I was with my buddy in his basement as he tried to figure out how to play his new Zeppelin record backward. Then we tried to "back mask" Petra to see if there were any hidden worship messages. (Let's face it, that would have been awesome.)

Now that's the crazier end of the spectrum. And I'm not going there. I don't want warnings about what we hear and what we see to cause us to be paranoid or legalistic. That's not the point *at all*. In fact, legalism, ironically, *is a way of obsessing about evil too*. And that's exactly the opposite of what I want us to do. But if anything, Christians today tend to be naive, which has too often left us unguarded.

Let's say you are incredibly anxious about an upcoming surgery. Your doctor can prescribe a sedative or have a musical therapist put together a relaxing playlist. Which do you choose? Then after the surgery, you are in extreme pain. Your doctor can give you a good dosage of morphine, or go with 80 percent of the dosage but also suggest some good tunes. Which do you assume would be more effective in relieving pain?

I'll give you my answers, but first let's go back to Proverbs, where immediately before telling us to guard our hearts, Solomon wrote this:

> My son, pay attention to what I say;
>  turn your ear to my words.
> Do not let them out of your sight,
>  keep them within your heart;
> for they are life to those who find them
>  and health to one's whole body.

PROVERBS 4:20–22

The words *listen* and *ear* (and similar expressions such as *pay attention* and *heed*) appear more than thirty times in Proverbs. Repeatedly we are instructed to be very careful about what we listen to.

Why?

Our ears are a pathway to our minds (or your *leb*!). What we hear pours in and shapes our thoughts, which then shape our lives.

There's a tendency to believe, *I don't need to worry about what I hear. The music I listen to on the radio, well, I'm not the one singing it. The comedian I listen to, yeah, I'm not the one telling the jokes. I mean . . . I haven't really done anything.* That's true; you haven't done anything. But something is being done *to you*.

For instance, do you think the music you listen to impacts your thinking? It does, more than you can imagine. Research proves that the music we listen to can promote health or lead to illness,[15] cause or alleviate depression,[16] influence spending and productivity,[17] and alter our visual perception of the world.[18] Other research suggests music can increase aggressive thoughts and encourage crime.[19]

And it turns out that prior to surgery, listening to a relaxing playlist created by a licensed music therapist leads to significantly lower anxiety levels than taking benzodiazepine sedatives,[20] while postsurgery patients who listened to music were shown to need 18.4 percent less morphine to dull their pain.[21]

Pay attention to what you listen to—and not just music but also podcasts, pundits, and other people's perspectives.

We'll talk more about this later in the book, but some of what our hearts hear the most are the words that come out of our own mouths.

## THE EYE-GATE

Right after telling us to guard our hearts, Solomon writes in Proverbs 4:25, "Let your eyes look straight ahead; fix your gaze directly before you." *Eye* or *eyes* is mentioned nearly thirty times just in the book of Proverbs, and the words *look* and *see* close to twenty times. Why? Because what we see pours into our minds.

The average American spends seven hours and four minutes looking at a screen each day. Worldwide the number is six hours and fifty-eight minutes.[22]

We want to believe, *C'mon, I can watch stuff. It's just looking*, but the Bible says (and modern research confirms) that when we open the gate, what flows into our hearts will flow out in our lives. The trash will make its way downstream.

What we let into the gates of our minds *matters*. And as a culture, we're not doing a very good job at guarding our hearts and minds. Recent research shows that "excessive screen usage has detrimental effects on social and emotional growth, including a rise in the likelihood of obesity, sleep disorders, and mental health conditions including depression and anxiety. It can obstruct the ability to interpret emotions, fuel aggressive conduct, and harm one's psychological health in general."[23]

What we watch with our eyes shapes the thoughts in our brains, and our thoughts shape our lives.

## THE CUMULATIVE EFFECT

One of the reasons we leave these gates unguarded is that the output coming from the input isn't immediately apparent. It happens a little at a time. Seeds get planted and slowly grow into thoughts that bear fruit in our lives.

Imagine going to the doctor and discovering that you've gained twenty pounds since your last visit. Your doctor asks, "How did that happen?"

The doctor is not expecting a date and time. "Well, everything was fine until last Thursday. We went to the buffet and, voila, twenty pounds!"

No. Your doctor knows something happened, *but it didn't happen all at once*. It may be difficult to identify what happened because it happened incrementally. There was a cumulative effect. Your intake of something changed, and the effects showed up little by little.

Almost everything—investing financially, doing drugs, eating Oreos—has a cumulative effect, and this certainly applies to what we hear and see. Listen to one angry song and it won't necessarily change your life. Keep listening to angry songs and you have to wonder why you've become an angry person.

Solomon writes, "Ears that hear and eyes that see—the LORD has made them both" (Proverbs 20:12). God made them both—for himself. He gave us ears and eyes to help us know and worship him and serve others.

## WHAT DO YOU NEED MORE EXPOSURE TO?

We need to demolish our strongholds. We don't use the weapons of this world, but instead we rely on God's power. This will be the major focus of section 3, but for now, remember that the law of cognition and the rule of exposure can work for you instead of against you. As we will see, the same dynamics that lead to us to being *conformed* can lead to us to being *transformed.*

My friend, who is a personal trainer, tells his clients who are trying to lose weight that it will take four weeks for them to notice changes in their body and eight weeks for their friends to notice. So if you're going to do it, you've got to do it for at least eight weeks. My experience is that if you get intentional with your exposure, you will start to see a difference in about two weeks, and your friends and family will start to pick up on it in a month.

How about you try to be more intentional with what you expose your mind to over the course of the next two weeks? Call it an experiment. Guard the gates. Set some screen-time limits, ask your digital assistant to play worship music, take a break from social media, and read your Bible every day. A multitude of Bible reading plans are available on the YouVersion app. At the end of a few weeks, evaluate whether the mere exposure effect is having any impact on your life.

The key takeaway is this: Your mind is like a garden, and your thoughts are the seeds. What you choose to plant through your daily exposures will determine what grows. Every image you see, every word you hear, every interaction you have is planting something. The question is, are you cultivating weeds of negativity, fear, and doubt, or are you nurturing seeds of faith, hope, and love?

Really pay attention to what you're feeding your brain. Ask yourself, *Is this exposure helping me become more like Christ? Is it moving me closer to the person God created me to be?*

Remember, transformation doesn't happen overnight. But with each conscious choice to expose ourselves to God's truth and goodness, we're creating new neural pathways that will lead to lasting change. Our minds are incredibly powerful, and by harnessing the rule of exposure, we can partner with God in the beautiful process of renewing our minds and transforming our lives.

Before moving on to the next section, take a few minutes to think about how the mere exposure effect is affecting your thoughts, which in turn impacts your emotions and behaviors. I'll give you several blank lines. Take a few minutes to think through questions like these:

1. What behaviors have I been trying to change?
2. What thoughts might be behind those behaviors?
3. Is "the rule of exposure" influencing my thinking?
4. Getting practical—do I consume content that is out of alignment with my personal convictions and beliefs? Can I connect the dots between the consumption of that content and the thoughts or behaviors I want to change?
5. Do I find some content acceptable that a few years ago would have been offensive? What is my present trajectory?

# THE FIVE PATTERNS

## *...to the patterns of this world...*

**T**he thoughts we think are not isolated events; they create intricate neural pathways in our brains that shape our lives in predictable ways. These pathways, or thought patterns, become the lenses through which we interpret the world and respond to it. In Romans 12:2, the apostle Paul warns us, "Do not conform to the pattern of this world, but be transformed by the renewing of your mind" (emphasis added).

The "pattern of this world" that Paul refers to can be understood as the pervasive thought patterns reinforced by our culture. Neuroscientific research has shown that repeated thoughts strengthen neural connections, making these patterns increasingly automatic and difficult to break. These culturally reinforced thought patterns can become deeply ingrained, shaping our perceptions, emotions, and actions, often without our conscious awareness.

However, the same neuroplasticity that allows these patterns to form also provides the key to breaking free from them. By consciously identifying and challenging these thought patterns, we can weaken the associated neural pathways and create new life-giving and God-honoring patterns.

In the following chapters, we'll explore five common thought patterns that the world around us constantly reinforces. We'll delve into the neuroscience behind how these patterns form and persist, and, most importantly, we'll learn biblical strategies for breaking free.

## CHAPTER 4

# THE PATTERN OF INSECURITY

## FROM INNER CRITIC TO IDENTITY IN CHRIST

took my wife to the Smoky Mountains for a little getaway and some light hiking. I *love* being outdoors, but I am not an experienced hiker. If you were to pass me on the trail, I'm the guy wearing Jordans and carrying a backpack that looks like a computer bag for the office . . . because it *is* my computer bag for the office.

We were on an isolated trail. We hadn't seen a single person when we heard a noise. About twenty feet in front of us a large black bear stepped out of the woods and onto the trail.

I'd heard about this kind of thing happening, but it somehow didn't seem real. I looked at my wife, who seemed fine. She had this quiet confidence that communicated, *I don't have to outrun the bear. I just have to outrun my husband.* We both knew she could do that.

My first thought was, *I have no idea what to do.* Then I began to think about what resources I had for protection. *Let's see, I have a computer bag, a Payday bar, a couple water bottles, a phone charger, and a journal.* None of which inspired much confidence.

I was trying to think of a way to MacGyver them into a weapon to protect us when I remembered I had my phone on me. I got it out and quickly searched, *What to do if you encounter a bear in the Smoky Mountains?* But because I was nervous, my hands were shaking and the question got autocorrected as *What to do if you encourage a bear in the Smoky Mountains?* Thankfully Google knew what I meant.

My wife interrupted me to ask, "Kyle, what are you doing? Get off your phone."

"I'm researching." It seemed obvious to me, but I explained, "I'm trying to figure out what to do in this situation."

She gave me a look of disbelief, but I know my strengths. Some men are experienced survivors; I'm a researcher. It's what I do. And, sure enough, in a matter of seconds I found an article on what to do in this situation. My confidence was starting to return. But then I read the advice. It said if the bear is attacking, do not run but instead stand your ground. It said if the bear knows you are there but is not attacking, make your presence known by talking loudly, clapping, and singing.

The bear was staring at us as I tried to think of a song—*what's the appropriate tune to use to serenade a bear?*

Moments earlier we were talking about my niece landing a role in the play *Annie.* So I had Annie on my mind, and the one song I know by heart from that musical came out. I started singing—loudly, as my research had suggested—"The sun'll come out, tomorrow. Bet your bottom dollar that tomorrow there'll be sun."

I tried to get my wife to sing with me, but she was playing more of the Miss Hannigan role. I sang the words as loudly as I could, trying to be an intimidating version of an adorable redheaded orphan. Thankfully, my singing seemed to be a natural bear repellant, and we somehow survived.

Looking back, I'll admit my thoughts in that moment were caught up in a pattern of insecurity. I compared myself to the bear and knew I wasn't strong enough to fight off the bear. I wanted to impress my wife so she'd think of me as a courageous protector, but my mind was overwhelmed by thoughts of insecurity and fear.

Admittedly, sharing this story as an example of a time I felt insecure doesn't require much vulnerability from me. Anyone would feel frightened and insecure when encountering a bear. I supposed it's my insecurity that makes me use a story like that. If I'm being honest, I would tell you I *often* feel that way. I try to project an image that I'm sufficient and equipped, capable and competent, but I regularly find myself encountering situations in which I feel inadequate and afraid of what other people think.

Almost every weekend before I step out to preach on a Sunday, I must take my thoughts captive. I take ten minutes by myself to break the pattern of insecurity with prayers and intentional Scripture meditation. Something will occasionally come up that prevents me from that routine, and when I start to preach, my mouth goes dry, my ears start to ring, and I break out into a cold sweat. Thoughts start running through my head. *I'm not prepared for this message. I don't deserve to be in this role. Someone else should be up here. There's so much at stake, and I'm gonna blow this opportunity.*

## INSECURE THOUGHTS LEAD TO ANXIOUS EMOTIONS

A *Wall Street Journal* article shared a study of five thousand adults over a two-year period that found that "the more hours logged on social media, the more the sense of well-being and happiness declined." The article also cited a study focused on several thousand teens that discovered the use of social media apps like Instagram and Snapchat directly correlated to feelings of isolation, anxiety, and inadequacy.[1] It turns out social media is a buffet of thoughts that feeds our insecurity, which leads to feelings of anxiety.

We've talked about how our thoughts shape our emotions, and how so much of the anxiety in our culture is connected to our thought patterns of insecurity. Here is what is happening cognitively: Our insecure thoughts often center around situations that feel threatening to our lives in some way, maybe threatening to our reputation, the future we've imagined, or the picture we have in our heads of what our lives and relationships look like. The brain's amygdala is where our emotions are processed, and our insecure thoughts trigger a stress response in the amygdala that makes us feel anxious.

Insecure thoughts often focus on potential problems or fears of future failure. In recent years, as I attended different leadership conferences, I've discovered something called "imposter syndrome." It describes thoughts that leaders often struggle with—feeling like a fraud, undeserving of the success they've had or the position they're in. Those thoughts often lead them to be anxious that they'll be revealed as an imposter. What's interesting is that research indicates that the imposter syndrome is especially common among high achievers. Therefore, the people you might think struggle with these thoughts the least often struggle with them the most.

## FINDING THE PATTERN

The pattern of insecurity typically looks something like this:

- caring excessively about what others think
- comparing ourselves unfavorably to others
- capitulating to negative thoughts and critical self-talk

As we expose the pattern of insecurity in our thinking, we'll see that it typically begins with excessively caring about others' opinions, which leads us to constantly compare ourselves to those around us. This comparison inevitably falls short, causing us to capitulate to negative self-talk and external pressures. This capitulation then reinforces our concern about others' opinions, and we find ourselves trapped in this cyclical pattern.

### Caring What Others Think

Why is the pattern of insecurity so common today?

Insecure thoughts may come from being perfectionistic, catastrophizing, listening to hypercritical voices, or a number of other factors, but there's no doubt that caring what others think is where a lot of our insecure thoughts begin.

A little more than a year ago I took an unplanned sabbatical. Initially, I looked forward to some time away, but because it wasn't planned and we didn't communicate the plan as well as we should have, rumors started. I wasn't prepared for that.

There were, of course, the typical rumors I'd expect, but probably my favorite was that I had plastic surgery and was taking time to recover. I loved that one because I'm sure the person who started it had something specific in mind. You know, something specific I needed to have fixed. *Kyle is finally taking care of . . .*

Some of the rumors were hurtful to me and my family. One day, I expressed frustration to a mentor friend. He encouraged me and told me it was inevitable in our suspicious, high-doubt culture, so I shouldn't take it personally.

I wasn't convinced.

I argued. "I know. I get it. But . . . but I don't want people to talk about me like I'm some sort of moral failure."

My friend immediately jumped in and said, "Well, let me stop you there. You *are* a moral failure."

I paused and then pooh-poohed him with, "Well, yeah, I know we're all moral failures, but you know what I mean."

"Kyle," he pushed back, "you *are* a moral failure. Your worry about what degree of moral failure people think you are reveals a fundamental misunderstanding of the gospel."

I knew he was right. My thoughts about what people think of me had created a pattern of insecurity. Proverbs 29:25 reads, "Fear of man will prove to be a snare, but whoever trusts in the LORD is kept safe." I had fallen into the trap of fearing what people thought of me.

Is it possible your insecurity is the result of caring what people think rather than trusting yourself to the Lord? In 1 Thessalonians 2:4, Paul wrote that living for Jesus means we stop seeking to please people and instead focus on pleasing God, who is the only one who knows our hearts. But the pattern of this world conditions us to do just the opposite.

The more caught up we are in what people think, the more self-conscious and egocentric we become, which only fuels further insecurity. One obvious place we see evidence of this is in our obsession with selfies. We take about 92 million selfies every day. The average person takes about 450 a year.[2] People are taking so many pictures of themselves that a new medical condition has emerged—selfie wrist. I wish I was kidding. An orthopedic surgeon describes it as a form of carpal tunnel syndrome in which hyperflexion of the wrist causes the nerve to become inflamed and angry.[3] People are taking so many selfies their wrists are fed up.

All these selfies seem to indicate obsessive thoughts about ourselves. It's not a coincidence that with the rise of selfies, we've seen a rise in cosmetic surgeries. Selfies and cosmetic surgeries have become so intertwined there's actually a term for it—"selfie surgeries." It's not surprising that thinking about ourselves and our appearance would lead to such dramatic measures because, as we keep seeing, our thoughts shape our lives and direct our decisions.

Research tells us it takes about eleven seconds to decide if we're satisfied with a selfie, but we will then spend another twenty-six minutes debating whether we should post it on social media.[4] Meanwhile the thought pattern of insecurity is becoming more and more established.

It's not just selfies. For decades, social scientists have been giving kids a list of sixteen values and asking them to rank them in order of importance. Year after year, "fame" was at or near the bottom. Then 2007 happened. What happened? *Keeping Up with the Kardashians* premiered on TV. Increasing opportunities to post online videos and status updates happened. And starting in 2007, "fame" jumped to the number one value of preteens.[5]

We could say these kids are egocentric, and perhaps they are, but is it possible that this egocentricity has been growing in a soil of insecurity? Perhaps the fear that *I'm not enough. I don't matter. I don't have what it takes* leads to thoughts of *If only I were famous, maybe then I'd get noticed instead of blending in and disappearing into the other eight billion people in the world.*

To be clear, it's not just kids. Adults struggle with feeling too small but camouflage these feelings by trying to appear big. Do you? It's another humble brag on Facebook. One more purchase you can't afford, so your life seems fuller than it is. Posting another pic on Instagram that gives the impression that you've got it all together.

That's how insecurity may present itself in your life. People may look at you and assume you are the *opposite* of insecure, but it's a facade. Inside, you're thinking, *I'm not enough. I'll never be enough. My life doesn't matter. I don't have what it takes.* But you keep singing for the bear.

## Comparing Ourselves to Others

Excessively caring about what people think leads us further into the pattern of insecurity, constantly comparing ourselves to others. Psychologists talk about social comparison theory—our tendency to determine our self-worth by how we compare ourselves to others.[6] God tells us it's not wise to compare ourselves with others (see 2 Corinthians 10:12), but we do it anyway, and it erodes our self-esteem.[7]

This is a toxic practice because we are comparing our actual lives with the best version of everyone else's lives. We used to just get glimpses into other people's lives—how our neighbor's yard looked and how nice a car they had in the driveway. Today, because of social media, we are flooded with the facade of the best version of our neighbor's life.

There are, of course, good things about social media. I'm not against it, but we need to understand that it's not real. It's about other people posting what they want us to see. Looking at it multiple times a day, we get the impression that everyone else has perfect kids, are always on vacation, and just bought brand-new cars.

I get it. We naturally post what we want other people to see. It would seem odd to do anything else. We would think it strange if someone posted, "I'm hating my kids today" or "I gained another two pounds this week" or "I'm pretty sure I'm the worst employee at my job. I should be fired."

No one does that.

When we scroll through social media, we are seeing idealized versions of people's lives, which will play on our insecurities. I hope you hear me, the posts and pictures you see making their lives seem perfect—it's *not* real. Without exception, every single person you see on social media is struggling.

Some studies have revealed when someone is having financial struggles, they're more likely to post pictures of themselves on a shopping trip. Or if they're having marital struggles, they're more likely to share posts about their romantic dates with their spouse.[8] Why? Because they don't want anyone to know. They want to hide their insecurities. But we see their posts and think, *My life isn't as good. I'm not as good. I'm not enough. I don't matter. I don't have what it takes.*

The danger is that we see these posts every day, which leads us to think these thoughts over and over, and so they can easily become mental ruts we find ourselves falling into all the time.

### Capitulating to Negative Self-Talk

Excessive caring and constant comparing leads to capitulating to negative thoughts and critical self-talk. We've created a neural pathway for the way we think of ourselves. Maybe the insecure thoughts we have about ourselves are stuck on repeat:

- I'm not enough.
- I can't do this.
- I don't have what it takes.
- I don't have the energy.
- My experience is insufficient.
- I am too sinful.
- Everyone else is more attractive than me.
- I never know what to say.
- My background is too messy.
- I don't have enough self-discipline.

It may sound different in your mind, but the underlying message is the same: You're inadequate, unworthy, or incapable. You may be plagued by thoughts like, *I don't really know what I'm doing. My kids would be better off with a different parent. No one appreciates me. Someday everyone's going to realize I'm not who they think I am. No matter how hard I try, I won't be good enough.*

These thoughts don't exist in isolation. They form a self-reinforcing loop that can dominate every aspect of our lives. Once we're in this pattern of thinking, here's how this insecurity loop typically plays out:

- **The trigger:** An event or situation challenges our sense of self-worth. It could be a work presentation, a parenting decision, or a simple scroll through social media.
- **The insecure thought:** Our go-to insecure thought springs to mind. *I can't do this. I'm not good enough.*
- **The emotional response:** This thought triggers feelings of anxiety, shame, or inadequacy.
- **The behavior:** Driven by these emotions, we might withdraw, over-compensate with arrogance, mask our insecurity with anger, or avoid challenges altogether.
- **The reinforcement:** Our behavior often leads to outcomes that seem to confirm our initial insecure thought. If we withdraw from a challenge, for instance, it only reaffirms our insecurity.

Let's look at how this might play out in different areas of life:

- **At work:** Our insecurity might whisper, *I'll never succeed or have the career I've dreamed about.* This thought leads to anxiety, causing us to hold back in meetings or hesitate to apply for promotions. As a result, we may be passed over for opportunities, which only reinforces our belief that we're not capable of success.
- **In personal growth:** When trying to break a bad habit, we might think, *Why even try? I know I can't do it.* This thought breeds

discouragement, leading us to give up before we've even started. Each failed attempt strengthens our belief in our lack of self-discipline and in our inevitable failure.

- **In parenting:** Every time one of our kids makes a bad decision, we feel like it's our fault. This thought pattern can lead to either overcompensating (becoming a helicopter parent) or withdrawing emotionally. Both responses can strain our relationship with our children, thereby confirming our fears about our parenting abilities.
- **On social media:** As we scroll through our favorite social media platforms, we might find ourselves whispering, *I'll never be that creative. I'll never be that fun. I'm never going to be that photogenic. I'll never be that spiritual.* These comparisons can lead to feelings of inadequacy, causing us to either present a false image online or withdraw from social connections. Both responses can increase feelings of isolation and inauthenticity, thus feeding back into our insecurities.

The insidious nature of this loop is that each cycle deepens the neural pathways associated with these insecure thoughts, making them more automatic and harder to challenge. Over time, this leads to a life dominated by anxious insecurity, where every experience is filtered through a lens of self-doubt and inadequacy.

Breaking this cycle requires more than just positive thinking or behavior change. It demands a fundamental rewiring of our thought patterns, replacing lies with truth and learning to see ourselves through God's eyes rather than the distorted mirror of our insecurities. It means building a new pattern of thought based on our true identity in Christ.

## I MATTER TO THE ONE WHO MATTERS MOST

Part of the difficulty with these negative thought patterns is that there's a hint of truth in all of them. The cultural approach to the pattern of insecurity would be to fill our minds with thoughts of self-worth and self-empowerment. To look at ourselves in the mirror and try to convince ourselves that we've got what it takes. We'll unpack this in the final chapters, but the biblical approach isn't to practice positive thinking until you believe something about yourself that isn't true.

Do you remember the Bible passage in which God calls Moses to come to a burning bush? He tells Moses he is sending him to stand in front of Pharoah, the most powerful ruler in the world, to demand the Israelites be set free from slavery in Egypt. I can only imagine the thoughts running through Moses's mind. There he is, standing shoeless in the desert where he served as a shepherd for his father-in-law. Moses immediately feels insecure and anxious. He has a list of reasons why this is a bad idea. You can hear the insecurity in his voice when he says to God, "Who am I, that I should go to Pharaoh and bring the Israelites out of Egypt?" (Exodus 3:11)

God doesn't reply, "Moses, you can do this. You're good enough and smart enough, and people like you." God simply says, "I will be with you" (Exodus 3:12). He directs the thoughts of Moses off of Moses and onto himself. When Moses tells God he thinks it's a bad idea because he's not a good speaker, God doesn't try to convince Moses otherwise. Instead, he gives Moses a different way to think about it. In essence, God tells Moses, "I made your tongue" (see 4:11).

I love the way the Amplified Bible renders Philippians 4:13: "I can do all things [which He has called me to do] through Him who strengthens and empowers me [to fulfill His purpose—I am self-sufficient in Christ's sufficiency; I am ready for anything and equal to anything through Him who infuses me with inner strength and confident peace]." The thought pattern of insecurity is interrupted by a new thought pattern: God's strength is sufficient, and his power available.

In his 1902 work titled *Human Nature and the Social Order*, Charles Cooley laid out the concept known as the "looking-glass self." He explains that our thoughts about ourselves are often determined by how we think other people think of us: "The thing that moves us to pride or shame is not the mere mechanical reflection of ourselves, but an imputed sentiment, the imagined effect of this reflection upon another's mind."[9] He makes the argument that our self-concept comes from what we believe the most important people in our lives think of us. The question then becomes, *Who is the most important person in my life and what does that person think of me?*

About ten years ago, I was going through a challenging time and struggling with feelings of insecurity. I was having a hard time tuning down the self-critical thoughts in my head. During this time, it just so happened that God nudged our church elders to end our elders meeting with a special prayer time for me. We walked into a small room that had been set up in advance. They invited me to sit in a chair in a corner of the room. With the lights down and my body facing the wall, I wasn't sure what would happen next.

I felt two hands on my shoulders. Someone was standing behind me. I heard the familiar voice of one of our elders speak into my ear. He spoke words of courage over me and prayed for me to know the power and presence of God. He walked away, and then there was another pair of hands on my shoulders. Another elder prayed and spoke over me: "God's strength is made perfect in your weakness, and his grace is sufficient. You can do all things through him who gives you strength."

One by one, they came and broke the pattern of insecurity that had been holding me captive. I didn't think any elders were left, but then one more person came behind me. I wondered who it was. I felt his hands on my shoulders. He bent over and spoke into my ear one word: "Son."

It was my dad. Without my knowledge, he had driven several hours to show up and be part of this moment. He spoke of his love for me and told me how proud he was of me. He reminded me that he was always in my corner. He prayed for me: "God, from one father to another, would you please remind our son how dearly he is loved and that with him we are well pleased."

Our deepest insecurities often stem from the place where we question our worth, our belonging, our identity. We wonder if we're truly loved, truly valued, truly enough. And no amount of positive self-talk can fully satisfy that deep longing for affirmation. Why? Because we were created to find our identity in relationship with our Creator.

Imagine for a moment. What if you could hear God's voice as clearly as

I heard my father's that day? What if you could hear him say, "My child, I am proud of you. I love you dearly. I am always in your corner"? How would that change the way you see yourself? How would those thoughts free you from excessively caring what others think? How would those thoughts help you let go of the constant comparisons?

Those thoughts are not simply wishful thinking. This is the reality of who we are in Christ. The Bible tells us that when we are in Christ, we are adopted as God's children (Ephesians 1:5). We have a Father who loves us unconditionally, who is always for us, who delights in us.

Breaking the insecurity loop isn't about mustering up more self-confidence or repeating positive mantras; it's about tuning our ears to hear the voice of our heavenly Father. It's about allowing his words of love and affirmation to sink deep into our hearts and overwrite the lies of insecurity with the truth of our identity in him.

Let his words of love and affirmation become the new soundtrack of your mind. You are loved. You are valued. You are enough—not because of anything you've done or failed to do, but because as a follower of Jesus, you are a child of God. Hear him whisper in your ear, "Son," or "Daughter," and let this truth fill your mind.

## CHAPTER 5

# THE PATTERN OF DISTRACTION

## FROM OVERWHELMED TO REFLECTIVE

One Friday before Christmas, my wife sent me to the grocery store with a list. It was bitterly cold outside, so I ran from my car to the store entrance. It was a crazy scene inside the store. It seemed that a lot of people were getting last-minute supplies for the holidays—or maybe just finding a warm place to take refuge from the frigid weather.

I grabbed a cart and quickly realized it was so crowded that people were loosely observing the typical "traffic laws" that civilized people follow to navigate through stores without a breakdown of order (or their sanity). I looked at my list. The first item seemed easy enough—*toothpaste*. I stayed in my lane and then exited into the health and beauty aisle and found . . . toothpaste pandemonium. A smorgasbord. Hundreds of varieties. (Or at least that's what it felt like.) My list said not just any garden variety of toothpaste, but Crest. I counted more than *twenty varieties* of Crest. My wife had specified even more—3D White Whitening Therapy Charcoal Deep Clean Toothpaste. *Wait, what?*

Don't get me started on the cheese section. Shocked and curious, I googled it—there are more than 1,800 cheese choices available these days if you live in a decent-size city. But as I did my research and tried to find the specific cheese my wife requested, some angry shopper behind me yelled, "Keep it moving, Grandma!" (Okay, fine, I added the "Grandma," but it was implied in the tone.)

I also had to buy cold medicine. I don't even wanna go there. Who knew? I saw *regular strength*, *severe strength*, and *extreme strength*. But also *extra strength* and *maximum strength*. I wonder why *regular* strength is even a thing. What psychopath feels sick and then goes out and buys regular strength cold medicine? The only legitimate purpose of regular strength is to make maximum strength look good. Regular strength is like the unattractive friend of maximum strength.

You get the point. You probably feel it too. Choice can be a curse sometimes. The thing is, this deluge of options isn't faced just at the grocery store. The choices for what to buy online are even more abundant—85 flavors of Oreos, 100 flavors of Pop Tarts, 7,500 varieties of apples—not to mention what to watch, play, and learn. We have some six thousand choices of movies or TV shows to watch on Netflix. And if that's not enough, we can tune into one of the other *two hundred plus* streaming services.

Not enough? You could try to conquer a video game. There are more than five million you can play.

Not enough? No problem, because there are about nine million apps you can download on your phone.

Again, *you get it*. This is your world too. And while we may love having options, this constant bombardment of choices can lead us down unexpected mental pathways. Our minds become overwhelmed and constantly distracted by the abundance of choices. And this is where the concept of cognitive biases come into play. Cognitive biases are like mental shortcuts our brains use to navigate the complexity of choices and to help us understand how distractions form thought patterns that affect our emotions and influence our decisions.

- **Complexity bias:** We prefer things that are complex and complicated, even if they are wrong or worse for us. Sociologist and researcher Renata Salecl asks, "How is it that in the developed world this increase in choice, through which we can supposedly customise our lives and make them perfect leads not to more satisfaction but rather to greater anxiety, and greater feelings of inadequacy and guilt?"[1] Studies have proven that abundant choices have not made our lives better, just more confusing.[2] In his book *The Paradox of Choice*, researcher Barry Schwartz explains we are at the point where "choice no longer liberates, but debilitates. It might even be said to tyrannize."[3] As Neil Postman put it, we are "amusing ourselves to death."[4] Another way you might say that is, *we are distracting ourselves to death.*
- **Attentional bias:** This bias helps explain how we filter the many distractions presented to us. We tend to give our attention to what we've given attention to in the past and to not consider other options or perspectives.
- **Negativity bias:** We give more attention to negative stimuli. Many of the distractions fighting for our thoughts are worrying or upsetting. Pay attention to the clickbait headlines that are vying for attention. You'll see titles like:
  - » *10 Everyday Foods That Are Slowly Killing You*
  - » *Why Your Retirement Savings Might Disappear Overnight*
  - » *Is Your Child Keeping a Dangerous Secret?*
- **Bandwagon bias:** This bias has to do with our tendency to believe or value things and filter distractions based on the practices and beliefs of the people around us.

## CARNIVAL OF CONTENT

Imagine going to a carnival where every attraction screams for your attention. The moment you step through the gates, you're assaulted by an array of sights and sounds. To your left, a roller coaster called the Headline

Hurl-a-Whirl. Breaking news comes at dizzying speed with nauseating effect. Constant ups and downs. The passengers want to get off and ride something different, but they're afraid they will miss something, so they stay on the roller coaster of constant news feeds.

Straight ahead, the social media carousel, called the Infinite Scroll, spins round and round in a blur of likes, shares, comparisons, and fleeting connections. It's an endless cycle of consumption that never stops spinning.

To your right is another ride called the Streaming Scream Machine. It's a ride that promises endless options of streaming shows and viral videos. Once someone hops on the ride, they have been known to disappear for days.

There's the haunted house of conspiracy theories, called the Paranoia Palace, where you spend hours letting your mind obsess over things that could potentially happen and get lost in a labyrinth of lies and half-truths.

As you keep walking through the carnival grounds, you come to the Buy It Now Bumper Cars. It's chaotic as you drive around, out of control, trying to bump into the latest "can't miss" deal of online shopping.

And then there's the Arcade, which is actually an arcade, where you can go in and play video games for hours. You assume it's full of middle school boys, but you're surprised when you walk in to find grown men in their thirties who haven't left the building since middle school.

You get the idea. Our minds are offered a carnival of content that offers us distractions and diversions. We spend our lives and our money riding the rides, losing track of time, and being blinded to what really matters. We've never had more access to things that can fill our minds, but its seems we've never been less mindful.

The challenge now is that the more *external input* we receive, the less *internal reflection* takes place. There's a connection between an excess of external input and an absence of internal reflection. We have more to think about, but we are thinking less about what matters.

All these distractions in our culture have given rise to what is sometimes called "the attention economy." Attention is a scarce commodity.

Businesses and content creators are continually competing for our limited cognitive resources. Sophisticated algorithms are designed to capture our attention and keep our focus. But what kind of impact does this pattern of thinking have on our minds, emotions, and relationships?

## THE NEUROSCIENCE OF DISTRACTIONS

We don't give much thought to distractions and the impact they can have on our brains. We've said that the prefrontal cortex is responsible for functions like focus and decision-making. And it works with the parietal cortex to decide what we will give attention to. This system works overtime these days because the constant stimuli of every ping, alert, vibration, and notification sends a signal that our attention is required.

Those tech wizards behind our favorite apps are basically neuroscience ninjas. They know that if their distractions can trigger a dopamine response, they have a good chance of getting our attention. Every time our phones buzz or a notification pops up, our brains go, *What's that? It could be something awesome!* That little rush of excitement is dopamine doing its thing. It's like our brains' own little party, and our screens are the DJs keeping the dopamine flowing. You know how it goes, one minute we're checking tomorrow's weather and the next we're deep into conspiracy theories about whether cats can actually read minds. (Spoiler: They totally can.)

All of these digital dopamine distractions are actually rewiring our brains. It's getting harder to sit still and focus on one thing. The more we indulge in these quick digital hits, the more our brains need to feel that same buzz. It's like needing extra sugar in our coffee to get the same kick. This might explain why some people find themselves diving deeper into porn than they ever planned. It's not just because they lack willpower; it's because of the brain chemistry that happens when we don't take our thoughts captive.

In his book *The Shallows*, Nicholas Carr calls the internet "a technology of forgetfulness" and describes that, because of the plasticity of our neural pathways, our brains are being rewired by digital distraction:

The more we use the Web, the more we train our brain to be distracted—to process information very quickly and very efficiently but without sustained attention. That helps explain why many of us find it hard to concentrate even when we're away from our computers. Our brains become adept at forgetting, inept at remembering.[5]

Brett McCracken writes about this kind of distraction as well:

Our rapid-fire toggling between spectacles—an episode of a Hulu show here, a Spotify album there—works against wisdom in the *moment*, by eliminating any time for reflection or synthesis before the next thing beckons. But it also works against wisdom in the *long term*, as brain research is showing. Our overstimulated brains are becoming weaker, less critical, and more gullible at a time in history when we need them to be sharper than ever.[6]

## THE EMOTIONAL TOLL OF A DISTRACTED LIFE

The pervasive pattern of distraction in our modern lives is taking a significant toll on our mental health. The constant barrage of notifications triggers our stress response, elevating cortisol levels and leaving us in a state of heightened anxiety. This perpetual connectivity has drastically reduced our time for introspection, leading to difficulties in emotional processing. Research increasingly points to a strong link between chronic distraction and depression. These frequent dopamine hits from our digital distractions can impair our brains' reward system, reducing our ability to feel pleasure, which can result in depression.

It's like our brains are running a never-ending marathon, processing cat videos and global news with equal vigor. And it has a way of leaving us feeling a bit—what's the word?—*meh*.

This pattern of distraction affects our minds and emotions, but especially our relationships with others. When my kids were younger, we were playing a game of charades as a family to enjoy some screen-free entertainment.

My middle daughter, Morgan, all of eight years old and bursting with energy, picks a card. Her eyes widen, a mischievous grin spreading across her face. The rest of us lean in, eager to guess. Morgan's tiny hands mime opening a laptop. Her face transforms, brow furrowing in exaggerated concentration. Her fingers fly over an imaginary keyboard, tap-tap-tapping with frenzied intensity. Her eyes, wide and unblinking, are fixed on an invisible screen.

A beat of silence. Then . . .

"DAD!" The room erupts in laughter and shouts of recognition. Everyone is in on the joke—but I'm not laughing. The laughter fades to background noise as the realization hits me like a punch to the gut. This is how my daughter sees me. This is the image I've burned into her young mind. Not playing hide-and-seek, not reading bedtime stories; instead, I am hunched over a glowing screen, lost in a digital world. What's worse, everyone knew instantly who she was imitating. It wasn't that I worked on a computer; *it was that this was the motion that defined me in her mind.*

In that moment, surrounded by the echoes of laughter, I knew I needed to fight to be free from this pattern of distraction. It was a wake-up call, delivered from the innocent hands of my eight-year-old daughter. It's an ironic twist that the digital distractions promising to connect us have actually left us more disconnected than ever.

Among many other negative things, the pattern of distractions leads to *fragmented conversations.* Our interactions are constantly interrupted, breaking the flow of dialogue and connection. However, there's a silver lining. The bar for attentiveness has been set so low that any effort to be fully present can make a significant impact. When we give someone our undivided attention, free from distractions, we communicate a level of value they may not be accustomed to receiving.

Have you heard of "phubbing"? It may sound risqué, but it's just slang for the act of snubbing someone in favor of your phone—a behavior so common we often don't realize we're doing it or having it done to us. This phenomenon has real consequences, as evidenced by a 2013 study published in the journal *Psychology of Popular Media Culture.* Researchers found that the mere presence of a mobile phone during a conversation, even when not in use, led to lower relationship quality and less closeness among participants.[7] This suggests that even the potential for distraction can negatively impact our connections.

This pattern of distractions also has a way of deeply affecting our existing relationships. This happens in all sorts of ways. One is by creating *empathy gaps*. When we divide our attention, we miss crucial emotional cues, making us less empathetic and emotionally engaged with the person we're trying to connect with. This lack of emotional attunement can lead to misunderstandings and a sense of disconnection. We all know what it feels like to have someone "miss us." It can be deeply hurtful, but let's be honest—the problem often simply began with distraction.

Another relational consequence is the loss of *meaningful moments*. This is so huge, and we shouldn't ignore it. When we are distracted, we often miss pivotal points in conversations without realizing it. This is particularly true for parents interacting with their children. Meaningful moments can arise unexpectedly, and our ability to recognize and seize them depends on our presence and engagement. We can be defined by what we *don't* say as much as what we *do*, and once these moments pass, they are gone forever.

Oof. Hard to think about, right? But we need to. And while we're on the topic, here's one more effect of distraction that's easy to overlook and hard to wrap our brains around: Present distractions rob us of *future memories*. When we're not fully present, we're not just missing out on the moment *then*; we're failing the future, as we're missing the opportunity to create lasting memories that keep us connected to our loved ones in the future. These shared experiences and memories are the building blocks of strong, enduring relationships that keep us connected.

We have to ask: Is the thing that is distracting us really worth all *this*?

## DISTRACTED INTO SPIRITUAL OBLIVION

In our modern bevy of options, it's the smartphone that is always pulling us in. Social media is shimmering like the fruit on the tree in Eden's garden. In this digital age, it is so easy to be "distracted from distraction by distraction" as T. S. Eliot wrote.[8]

We live in a culture marked by a pattern of distraction. This culture is always trying to squeeze us into its mold. In this culture, we make our to-do lists and plan out our weeks and check our calendars.

- We spend, on average, two and a half hours a day on social media.[9]
- We spend, on average, nearly four hours each day watching television.[10]
- All told, worldwide, the average person spends six hours and forty minutes looking at a screen.[11]
- We touch our phones on average . . . are you ready for this . . . 2,617 times a day.[12]

And in this culture, many Christians routinely say they just don't have time to pray or read the Bible and will show up at church maybe one Sunday a month.[13]

We incur all kinds of costs from being distracted, but perhaps the most insidious (but often inconspicuous) cost is to our spiritual lives. Theologian Ronald Rolheiser wrote (back in 1999, before the onset of social media and streaming services) that we "are distracting ourselves into spiritual oblivion."[14] And as we've seen already in this book, it is from the spiritual reality—of the *leb*, the heart and mind—that all the other problems spring.

In *The Screwtape Letters*, C. S. Lewis imagines a conversation between two demons in which Screwtape (an experienced demon) is mentoring Wormwood (a rookie demon) on how to keep people (which he calls "patients") from God (who he calls "the Enemy") and the life he has for them. Screwtape instructs Wormwood on the importance of distraction:

> I once had a patient, a sound atheist. . . . One day, as he sat reading, I saw a train of thought in his mind beginning to go the wrong way. The Enemy, of course, was at his elbow in a moment. Before I knew

where I was I saw my twenty years' work beginning to totter.... I struck instantly at the part of the man which I had best under my control and suggested that it was just about time he had some lunch.[15]

Screwtape instructs young Wormwood to train his patient to be distracted, encouraging him that eventually, "you will find that anything or nothing is sufficient to attract his wandering attention."[16]

The point is to not regard the internet, social media, TV, video games, and our phones as evil in and of themselves, but to understand that they can all be deadly weapons in the hands of Satan. He knows he doesn't have to get us to worship him or hate God. Those are hard sells. He can keep it simple and pull us away from everything that's truly important by keeping us focused on things that truly aren't. Distractions can derail our spiritual lives and even lead to our ultimate destruction.

## DISTRACTED BY THE GOOD

In Luke 10, we see Jesus and his disciples at a town called Bethany—a few miles outside of Jerusalem. They decide to stop and visit some close friends—sisters Mary and Martha and their brother Lazarus.

We don't know the birth order, but my guess is that Martha was the oldest; she's got some firstborn energy. Mary seems like a middle child. Lazarus might have been the younger brother. The parents just couldn't agree on an M name for him, and so they became Martha, Mary, and . . . Lazarus.

Luke writes, "As Jesus and his disciples were on their way, he came to a village where a woman named Martha opened her home to him" (Luke 10:38). How did she know they were coming? She probably didn't. Jesus likely is stopping by their home unannounced with at least his twelve disciples, but often others traveled with Jesus . . . so, maybe more people. Suddenly, Martha knows a lot of things need to happen.

A *lot.*

Thirteen—maybe dozens—of visitors. I can imagine her thoughts racing. *Is the house clean? Where will they all sit? What will they eat? Do we have enough LaCroix?*

It's a crazy situation. How would you feel if Jesus and maybe twenty people showed up right now, unannounced, at your house to hang out?

Martha is feeling it and gets to work.

Martha is joined in the work by . . . no one.

"She had a sister called Mary, who sat at the Lord's feet listening to what he said" (Luke 10:39). Martha runs to the kitchen, while Mary sits down—criss-cross, applesauce—on the living room floor, giving her full attention to Jesus.

Don't miss the significance of this. In that day, a woman sitting at the feet of a rabbi would have been unheard of. People would have seen this act of letting her sit at his feet as Jesus accepting her as one of his students, as someone he was preparing to carry on his mission. It might have been uncomfortable for everyone else—this was not in keeping with their tradition. But Jesus *loved* it. This was a special moment. It was not to be missed. But it was being missed, by someone who surely would have loved to be on that floor too.

"But Martha," Luke goes on, "was distracted by all the preparations that had to be made" (Luke 10:40). Mary sits at the feet of Jesus in the living room. Martha peels potatoes and stirs lemonade in the kitchen.

I wonder *why* Martha is doing what she's doing. Was it out of a concern for Jesus and his disciples? If so, you could call it a form of worship. Or was it out of a concern for what people might think of her if she wasn't hard at work or if her house isn't clean enough or her food good enough. We don't know, but I do know it's easy to be driven by the fear of what other people think.

But we're just too quick to throw Martha under the bus. She was serving. I'm pretty sure God gives a thumbs-up to service. She was practicing hospitality. She wasn't in the kitchen scarfing down all the chicken nuggies before anyone else could eat any. She wasn't slandering a neighbor back behind the house. She wasn't committing lasciviousness (I admit I don't know what that is, but pretty sure I've seen it in the Bible and that it's not good).

At the very least we can say that what distracts Martha isn't *bad*. In fact, what distracts her from Jesus is *good*. Hospitality is wonderful, and she is showing love, right? Absolutely. *But that doesn't mean she still isn't missing out*. That's the thing about distractions—they can be good and still keep us from what is *best*.

Martha isn't doing anything bad.

She also isn't doing anything neutral. It isn't that Jesus is teaching in the family room and she is in the kitchen scrolling through Instagram or in her bedroom binge-watching old *Bridgerton* episodes.

What Martha is doing is *good*.

It just isn't *best*.

Doing something good can be a bad choice when there's something better that needs our attention.

The Bible uses a word to describe what Martha was doing. Did you catch it? *Distractions*. Mary sat at Jesus' feet listening to everything Jesus said, but "Martha was distracted." Good things that take us away from better things are "distractions." Martha was distracted by good things, which made her miss out on something better—Jesus.

Martha becomes annoyed with her sister and then seems a little annoyed with Jesus. "She came to him and asked, 'Lord, don't you care that my sister has left me to do the work by myself? Tell her to help me!'" (Luke 10:40). She wants her sister to do what she's doing and assumes Jesus is on her side. Yeah, we need to be careful about assuming Jesus is on our side, because Jesus is always on Jesus' side.

"'Martha, Martha,' the Lord answered, 'you are worried and upset about many things, but few things are needed—or indeed only one. Mary has chosen what is better, and it will not be taken away from her'" (Luke 10:41–42). Jesus tells Martha that while she may have chosen what's good, Mary chose what's better.

## THREE WORDS AND ONE THING

Three adjectives in the text describe Martha—*distracted*, *worried*, *upset*. (The word *upset* can also be translated "easily annoyed.")

Could *distracted* describe you?

How about *worried*?

Are you *easily annoyed*?

Perhaps you wouldn't use these words to describe yourself, but if I asked the people you do life with, would they smile and say, "Is this off the record?"

Our culture has a pattern of distraction, and as we've seen, the research conducted by psychologists and sociologists say our worry and annoyance may be the fruit that grows on the tree of distraction, which has its roots in our culture of choices and complexity.

We've never had access to more information. I read that we now produce more content in two days than all the information from the beginning of time until the year 2003—but we're more anxious than ever.[17]

We've never had more opportunities for connection with our technology and social media, but it's left us strangely disconnected and divided, increasingly lonely and upset with each other.

*One thing is needed.*

I love the simplicity of Jesus' response to Martha. *What you're doing is good, Martha, but there's one thing that's always better, and it's spending time with me.* Practicing the presence of Jesus is always better.

Part of me reads that and wants Jesus to say a bit more. *Jesus, don't you want to say more? I mean, yes, that is better, but . . . there is other stuff we have to do. Don't you want to mention that?*

Nope.

"Few things are needed—or indeed only one. Mary has chosen what is better."

## ELIMINATE SOME DISTRACTIONS

Recently, we celebrated the Lord's Supper at church on a Sunday morning, and I was sitting in the pew, holding the bread and juice, praying silently, *Lord, I want to thank you for your sacrifice. Thank you for dying on the cross so my sins could be forgiven. I love you. Nothing means more to me than*

*my relationship with you. I'm sorry I missed some time with you this week.*
Something about the word *missed* connected my brain to trash day a few
days earlier.

I had missed trash day, and I began to think, *I don't understand why
the garbage collectors can't come at a more consistent time. I don't think they
were early this time, but sometimes they come early, and I haven't gotten it out
yet. Maybe I need to take the trash out the night before. How do I remember
to do that? I guess I should just schedule it on my calendar. Oh yeah, I need
to go in and get my driver's license renewed this week. I guess I could go on
Wednesday. But that's the day* . . . which is when my wife gently nudged me.
I guess more accurately I could say she painfully pinched me. I looked over,
annoyed, but I saw the look on her face that said, *Put your phone away; it's
Communion time.*

Oh.

I hadn't done it on purpose, but I had my phone in my right hand and
the elements in my left.

*Wow.*

Talk about distracted. I wasn't taking my thoughts captive, and here
I was, a *pastor*, and I was diluting a moment of holiness. I was so grateful
for that gentle nudge.

If you've been around church much, you've likely heard a lot about
repenting of your sins but little about eliminating distractions. Yes, sin
is bad, but as Screwtape taught Wormwood, it's easier to get a Christian
distracted, and it can all lead to the same place. If we don't do something
drastic about all the distractions, it will be very difficult to be the kind of
person who sits at the feet of Jesus. We can be doing something good and
still miss the heart of it all. We can be missing what is best.

## NEVER TAKEN AWAY

Jesus said of Mary, "She has chosen what matters most, and it won't be
taken from her." The verb tense of "it won't be taken" in the original language is better rendered "it will *never* be taken." It will last forever.

Devoting our time to relationships—to truly loving God and other people—is the one thing we can do with our time here on earth that will last for all of eternity.

So sit at his feet.

I can't help but wonder how the story ends. We're not told. Jesus says to Martha, "You're worried and upset about many things, Mary has chosen what is better." That's it.

Part of me wonders if Martha shook her head in disbelief and went back to work. *Whatever. Somebody's got to do all this work.* But I hope Martha paused, took off her apron, assumed her criss-cross applesauce spot next to Mary, and put her focus on Jesus.

I don't know if that happened. I know it's hard to do. It takes a commitment to defy the pattern of distraction. It takes resolve to stick to that commitment. It won't be easy, but you'll never regret it because *Jesus* is what's better, and sitting at his feet will last forever.

Breaking free from the pattern of distraction begins by not being distracted from its reality in our lives. But how do we practically defy this pattern in our daily lives? Like Mary, we want to be intentional with our attention and focus on what truly matters. In subsequent chapters, we will get even more practical, but for now, let's consider some concrete steps to help us break free from the pattern of distraction:

- **Digital detox:** Begin by setting boundaries with your devices. Designate specific times each day as screen-free zones. This might mean no phones at the dinner table, no screens an hour before bedtime, or a "tech Sabbath" one day a week. The goal is to create space for undistracted thought and genuine human connection.
- **Mindful consumption:** Be intentional about what you allow into your mental space. Before consuming any content, ask yourself, *Is this enriching my life or merely distracting me?* (The *this* applies to social media, news, entertainment, and even conversations.)
- **Single-tasking:** In a world that glorifies multitasking, commit to

doing one thing at a time. When you're working, work. When you're resting, rest. When you're with loved ones, be fully present. This practice helps retrain your brain to focus deeply rather than flit among superficial engagements.

- **Regular reflection:** Set aside time each day for quiet reflection—through praying, meditating on Scripture, or simply sitting in silence. Use this time to process your thoughts, connect with God, and refocus on what's truly important.
- **Environmental design:** Create a physical environment that supports focus. This may mean having a dedicated workspace, using noise-canceling headphones, keeping your phone outside of your reach while you're in bed, or simply clearing clutter from your desk. Your external environment can significantly reduce your distractions.
- **Accountability:** Share your commitment to defying distraction with a trusted friend or family member. Ask them to check in on your progress and offer support when you struggle.

Remember, defying distraction is not about achieving perfect focus all the time; it's about reclaiming your attention, one step at a time, and aligning it with your values and God's purpose in your life. It's a journey of small, consistent choices that, over time, reshape your mental landscape.

As you implement these strategies, be patient with yourself. You're undoing patterns that have been reinforced by our culture for years. Celebrate small victories. Did you make it through a meal without checking your phone? That's progress. Did you complete a task without toggling among multiple browser tabs? That's a win.

The commitment to defy distraction is ultimately a commitment to live more fully—to be more present, more intentional, and more aligned with God's will for your life. It's about creating space for the still small voice of God to be heard amidst the noise of our world.

As we move forward, remember the words of Hebrews 12:1–2: "Let us throw off everything that hinders and the sin that so easily entangles. And let us run with perseverance the race marked out for us, fixing our eyes on Jesus." In our context, the distractions of this world are often what hinder and entangle us. By consciously choosing to fix our eyes on Jesus instead, we can break free from the pattern of distraction and run our race with purpose and clarity.

## CHAPTER 6

# THE PATTERN OF OFFENSE

## FROM TRIGGERED TO TRANSFORMED

I never thought I'd become the kind of person who was easily offended. Ironically, the one thing that often offended me was people who were easily offended. As a pastor, I prided myself on my thick skin and soft heart. I thought I knew how to handle criticism gracefully. But somewhere along the way, things changed.

It started small—a critical comment about my sermon here, a staff member's cynical question there. Normally, I would have brushed off these instances, but they began to stick. Each perceived slight felt like a personal attack, and I found myself dwelling on them long after I should have let them go. This pattern of offense can have a compounding effect, where one offense builds on another.

I was starting to feel I had the spiritual gift of disappointing people. No matter how hard I tried, I felt like I couldn't meet expectations. The constant scrutiny made me sensitive and defensive. And lonely.

My wife noticed the change. "What happened to the man who used to always keep things in perspective and assume the best in people?" she asked one evening.

"What's that supposed to mean?" I shot back, not keeping perspective and assuming the worst. Her words stung because I knew they were true. When most people offended me, I had to hold a smile and keep a steady tone. Increasingly those offenses were piling up and getting transferred onto her and my kids.

## THE AGE OF RAGE

You may have noticed that people out there are pretty angry. Everyone is offended—from attendees at HOA meetings in nice suburban neighborhoods to political pundits on TV, to sports fans on talk radio, to friends on social media, to the person driving beside me right now who seems annoyed that I'm voice recording this paragraph into my phone.

It seems people have never been more easily offended, and these thoughts of offense have led to a national outbreak of anger. Check out these headlines:

- "The Age of Rage"[1]
- "Is Our Society Getting Increasingly Angry?"[2]
- "Why Is Everyone So Angry? We Investigated"[3]
- "Soothing Advice for Mad America"[4]
- "A Recent Rise in Rage. Why Are We So Angry?"[5]
- "Americans Are Living in a Big Anger Incubator"[6]
- "The Real Roots of American Rage"[7]

It's our culture. And it seemingly keeps getting worse. Why are people so quick to get offended and angry?

- **Increased awareness:** We are increasingly exposed to issues that get us worked up. The news channels run stories twenty-four hours a day, and the notifications on our phones are incessantly pinging us with alerts of things happening that should upset us.

- **Social media amplification:** Online platforms can magnify and spread outrage quickly. Our algorithms know we won't keep scrolling if we see something that upsets us or feels like a threat.
- **Echo chambers:** With polarized news and friend groups, people can choose to almost exclusively be exposed to like-minded views, which makes us even more intolerant of people who disagree with us or have different opinions.
- **Victim competition:** There seems to be an unspoken competition over who has been most offended. If we assign personal value to the degree of victimization we face, we will be constantly looking for offense.

That's the culture we live in—one that is trying to squeeze us into its mold. If we're not careful, we'll get woven right into the pattern of offense. And don't be offended by this, but . . . I wonder if you already have.

## CABIN PRESSURE

Anger is everywhere, but one particular place where people are taking offense is at about thirty thousand feet. We might call it sky-high sensitivity. Travel is stressful, after all.

As I took my seat on the plane, the woman next to me looked at me like she was sitting beside Hitler. She gave a heavy grunt of offense, but I had no idea what I had done. I thought maybe she was just hoping to have an empty seat next to her. But contempt filled every word of the question she attacked me with: "Are you wearing cologne?"

She was upset, and I wasn't sure how to respond. I nodded and meekly said, "Yes," hoping that was right answer. It wasn't.

Her back arched and (I'm pretty sure) her claws came out as she hissed, "I'm allergic."

I smelled so good I offended her. I found myself apologizing for smelling like apple sandalwood.

I will admit, it's not always the other passengers who are annoyed. I've been known to take offense a few times myself. I was waiting at the airport to board a three-hour direct flight to Denver. Things weren't looking good: I was on an economy airline that doesn't offer much legroom and has seats that don't recline—and I was in a middle seat. All of this is a recipe to be easily offended. While we were waiting to board, I saw a guy with a dog and immediately thought, *It could be worse. I could be flying with no legroom in a middle seat that doesn't recline—and with a dog.*

I boarded the plane, hoping the person next to me would have a small frame, perhaps a child who was perfectly healthy but looks a little malnourished. I sat in my middle seat, with no one sitting next to me, thinking the boarding process was done. *Could that seat be open?* That's when the guy with the dog came around the corner. "Surely not," I whispered out loud. With each step, I prayed increasingly desperate prayers. Then he sat down next to me. Within thirty seconds, his dog was sitting *on my feet.* I am not exaggerating. I have pictures to prove it!

The man seemed oblivious. He started asking questions about why I was going to Denver. He told me about the Airbnb where he was staying and about a childhood injury that kept him from skiing, but never mentioned anything about *his dog sleeping on my feet.* Finally, he acknowledged the presence of his dog and tried to break the tension by saying, "Just to let you know, she gets a little gassy on flights. So it's her, not me." My guess is that it was him, not her, but either way: *Bro, get your dog off my feet!*

## THE ALCHEMY OF ANGER

Setting aside the airplane nightmares, can we be honest for a minute? Being offended kind of feels *good.*

No one wants to admit it. We complain loudly when wronged and act like someone just stabbed us in the eye with a fiery hot poker. But the truth we won't admit is that we kind of *enjoy* being offended. Why? Believe it or not, there are some neurochemical explanations.

Surprisingly, being offended triggers a dopamine release. You'll recall that dopamine is the feel-good chemical our brains release when we experience something pleasurable. Why is it activated by being offended? The best guess is that it's because of the anticipation of social reward when we share our offense with others and get their validation and attention.

When we are offended and get angry, the brain also releases stress hormones, such as cortisol, to respond to a situation that might be a threat. It's a survival tactic that surely came in handy in past centuries when everyday life was a little more ... stabby. Cortisol is a gift in the right situation, helping us respond quickly and decisively and activating our ability to fight or get the heck out of there. But when we're not actually in an emergency, the story is different, even if the chemical is the same. But one side effect is that it sort of feels *good*. Some people can become addicted to the rush of cortisol. They will even seek out situations that trigger it, where they take on risks or put themselves in danger.

But as if these chemicals aren't enough, there's more. When we share our offense with like-minded friends, it can increase our sense of social bonding with them, which leads the brain to release oxytocin—the "love hormone."

Being offended can also reinforce our self-identity, which triggers a complex interplay of neurotransmitters associated with self-affirmation. If we're proud and want to feel better, then getting angry will boost up our pride. If we think of ourselves as victims, then being offended reinforces our victim identity.

Unconsciously, the pattern of offense can become self-reinforcing. Each time we experience a good feeling that is associated with it, our brain's reward pathway is strengthened. We start *looking* for potential offenses.

As our thoughts dwell on offense, it has a way of snowballing. As the snowball of offense rolls down the hill of life, it picks up more offenses and has a way of turning into an avalanche of anger that causes all kinds of unintended destruction. You see, while the chemicals in the brain feel good, offense and conflict *don't*, not in the long term. In fact, they can lead us down a very dangerous path indeed.

## FROM SLIGHT TO SPITE

Taking offense may not be sin, but it can easily lead to anger, which will likely lead to sin. That's why Paul issues a warning: "'In your anger do not sin.' Do not let the sun go down while you are still angry, and do not give the devil a foothold" (Ephesians 4:26–27).

Paul tells us to not let anger spend the night. The way we achieve that is by taking our thoughts captive when we are offended. A small seed of offense has a way of growing into bitterness. Once bitterness takes root, all kinds of weeds begin to bloom.

There is a particular thought that can keep us caught up in the pattern of offense: *If I ignore it, it will go away.* Proverbs 19:11 tells us to "overlook an offense," which means we recognize it and decide to let it go. *Ignoring* is different. It's a form of avoidance that only causes the offense to feel *more* offensive.

### A PARABLE: THE TALE OF TWO NEIGHBORS

In a peaceful village, there lived two neighbors, Vexanna and Erron. Each tended to their own flower garden, separated by a stone wall that stood no more than two feet off the ground. Vexanna kept her rose garden meticulous, while Erron enjoyed a more natural garden filled with a variety of flowers. Though Vexanna could be easily upset when things didn't go just right and Erron was sometimes careless, they enjoyed being neighbors and admired each other's gardens.

One windy day, Vexanna noticed a single dandelion growing on Erron's side of the wall. She watched in horror as the wind blew the seeds off that dandelion. Her eyes followed one single seed that made it across the wall and landed in her garden, right at her feet. She was mildly annoyed but chose to ignore it. As the days passed, she watched it carefully, and sure enough, where the seed had landed a dandelion grew and, along with it, Vexanna's irritation. One morning, she walked out, and there, among her perfect roses, stood a dandelion. A white puffball of seeds. She walked over to examine it. She got down on the ground and looked at it closely.

She could hear Erron working in his garden, whistling the same song he always whistled: "Always Look on the Bright Side of Life" from his favorite Monty Python movie. In the past she had never minded it, even thought it was somewhat charming, but today she found his whistling intolerable. Without saying a word, she marched inside and slammed the door. Erron was a bit startled when the door slammed. Later that day, he saw Vexanna outside and asked her if everything was okay. She was staring at the dandelion in her rose bushes as she responded with a terse, "Everything is fine."

Vexanna kept her eye on that dandelion, its fluffy seed head seeming to mock her every time she stepped outside, threatening to spread more seeds. Sure enough, after a number of days the seeds had blown off and spread among her roses. Soon her rose garden had at least a dozen dandelions. When Erron noticed the dandelions, he asked Vexanna if he could help her pull them from her garden. She rolled her eyes and walked away, vowing that she'd only work in her garden early in the mornings so she wouldn't have to see Erron. Vexanna began staying inside most days. Occasionally, she would look out her window, but the sight of Erron casually tending to his wild garden made her even more vexed.

One morning, she woke up furious. She had had enough. She got on her riding lawn mower and mowed down her once beautiful rose garden. While she was at it, she mowed down Erron's garden as well. She spent the day building the rock wall between their properties tall enough that she wouldn't be able to look over the top.

If you ride your bike by Vexanna's house today, you'll see that her yard has been overtaken by weeds and dandelions, but if you listen closely, you'll probably be able to hear Erron whistling, "Always Look on the Bright Side of Life" as he works in his new garden of sunflowers.

It started as a seed that turned into a weed that at any time could have been picked and thrown away. But instead, the days passed, the seeds spread, and the weeds took root.

Think through some of the thoughts that keep us from dealing with our feelings of offense. I'll give you several blank lines so you'll have a few minutes to do this exercise. As you read these reflections, see if you can match some of them to certain situations in your life:

- *If I don't get offended, it means I don't care about the issue. The more offended I am, the more it shows I care.* (These statements equate offense with conviction and are especially popular during election season.)
- *If I overlook what they said, they'll get away with it.* (This thought is rooted in the fear of being hurt again or being seen as weak.)
- *If I don't stay angry, then they won't have to pay for what they did.* (This conclusion assumes that resentment hurts them more than it hurts you. Spoiler alert: It doesn't.)
- *I'll stop being upset when they choose to apologize.* (This puts your emotional well-being in someone else's hands.)
- *If I don't get offended and upset, it means I'm weak.* (Someone taught you to think of forgiveness and graciousness as weakness. It's not. Try it.)
- *This offense is part of who I am.* (You've allowed someone other than God to give you your identity.)

## REFRAMING OFFENSIVE THOUGHTS

In Matthew 18:15 (NLT), Jesus addresses how to respond when some-one says or does something hurtful or offensive: "If another believer sins against you, go privately and point out the offense. If the other person lis-tens and confesses it, you have won that person back." Jesus says in cases of offense against us, we should go at once. We should be clear and specific about what offended us. In general, we should do it privately and with a spirit that desires reconciliation.*

---

* It's important to note that this verse addresses general interpersonal conflicts and minor offenses and is not intended to apply to situations of abuse, severe trauma, or criminal behavior. In such cases, safety is the primary concern, and professional help and/or legal intervention may be necessary. *Offense* in this context refers to personal slights, misunderstandings, or relational conflicts that don't involve physical, emotional, or spiritual abuse. When approaching any conflict,

Can I just point out what Jesus *doesn't* say to do if someone offends us:

- Immediately post a vague, passive-aggressive comment on social media.
- Tell lots of people about it and call it a "prayer chain."
- Find a Bible version that translates "turn the other cheek" as "roll your eyes."
- Rehearse witty comebacks in the shower for the next three weeks.

When an offense takes root, it grows into various weeds in our garden that can be difficult to pull up. After Paul warns us about sinning in our anger, he goes on to say, "Get rid of all bitterness, rage and anger, brawling and slander, along with every form of malice" (Ephesians 4:31). Did you notice the first four words of that verse: "Get rid of *all*"?

It would nice if he had said *some* instead of *all*. If I were Paul, I might have written, "Get rid of all anger, *except* acceptable anger," and then come up with a list of things that we *are* allowed to be offended by—talking on the phone during a movie, taking up two parking spaces, hitting "Reply All" when it only needs to be sent to one person, leaving time on the microwave without clearing it, double-dipping chips at a party, using ALL CAPS in text messages, constantly responding with emojis. I'm sure you could make your own list. Some offenses are hard to let go of because they are small and continual, and others are hard to let go of because they feel big and overwhelming.

Paul tells us to get rid of *all* anger. So, what do we do if someone offends us and makes us mad? Heed Ephesians 4:32: "Be kind and compassionate to one another, forgiving each other, just as in Christ God forgave you."

You will have times when your instant, knee-jerk reaction is to be offended and get angry. But you have to rid yourself of that anger, just like

---

wisdom, discernment, and sometimes professional guidance are crucial. The goal is always healing and reconciliation when possible, but not at the expense of anyone's safety. If you're unsure about how to handle a particular situation, seek counsel from a trusted pastor, therapist, or counselor.

you would get rid of a cancerous tumor in your body. Get rid of *all* your anger. Do not let it linger until bedtime. Don't sleep on it. Anger is not for you. Replace your anger with kindness, compassion, and forgiveness, just as God replaced his anger toward your sin with kindness, compassion, and forgiveness in Christ.

With the power of the Holy Spirit, we can live above the pattern of offense almost everyone else in our culture seems to be shaped by.

## THOUGHT STOPPING

What should we do when someone mistreats us and leaves us feeling offended? We don't focus on the feeling. Instead we are challenged by the words of Jesus' half-brother James: "My dear brothers and sisters, take note of this: Everyone should be quick to listen, slow to speak and slow to become angry, because human anger does not produce the righteousness that God desires" (James 1:19–20).

Anger doesn't produce the righteousness God has for us—the righteousness Jesus died for, so that we could live in it. Sometimes we have to choose between being right and being righteous. In those moments, we must be quick to listen, slow to speak, and slow to become angry.

We may agree with all that (or we may not), but once our fuse gets lit, it's hard to put it into practice. Why? Because of that frustrating, marvelous, divinely created brain of ours. When something happens that makes us angry, the little walnut-shaped part of the temporal lobe section of our brains called the amygdala fires up.

At the same time, an enhancement of activity takes place within the dorsal part of our pons, as well as a reduction of activity in our visual occipitotemporal cortex and our attentional parietal cortex, and our systolic blood pressure increases.[8] This stress response triggers our hypothalamic-pituitary-adrenal axis, which releases cortisol and adrenaline into our system. Our prefrontal cortex will try to engage to interpret the situation, but its rational decision-making is often overwhelmed by the biological thunderstorm created by our emotional response to the situation.[9]

Now those are a lot of big words. How can I say this in a less sciencey way? You lost it. Flew off the handle. Blew a gasket. Hit the roof. Went off the deep end. Had a meltdown. Popped your cork.

You were quick to listen, slow to speak, and slow to become angry—until you *weren't*. Things were fine until your buttons got pushed and you got offended. Once you got angry, your brain was not telling you to stop and think; it was telling you it's time to fight or flee. That's a good thing, of course, *if you need it*. But survival strategies are often too intense for most of our everyday situations. *That's where taking our thoughts captive comes in.*

Being quick to listen, slow to speak, and slow to become angry may feel impossible in the moment, but it turns out that God gave us some biological help with this. When that fight-or-flight mechanism kicks in, a part of the orbital frontal cortex, a part of the brain just above our eyes, gets engaged and serves the purpose of putting the brakes on our fired-up emotions. That's why, according to Darin Dougherty, a professor of psychiatry at Massachusetts General Hospital who studies this stuff, "Healthy people experience anger, but they can suppress it before acting on it."[10] In other words, they can stop and think.

To help us capture these angry thoughts and replace them with thoughts that are obedient to Christ, I want to give us one word to remember when we start losing our temporal lobe. The word is *stop*.

Stop.

If you're "a picture is worth a thousand words" kind of person, you might imagine a stop sign. When you start to feel angry, think of the word *stop*, or picture in your head the image of a stop sign.

This strategy is rooted in Scripture. It's a way to apply our key verse—to take our runaway, self-destructive, harmful thoughts captive. And it's also confirmed by modern research. If you were to go to an anger management course, one technique they teach is called "thought stopping." What is that? "Thought stopping prevents unwanted and unpleasant thoughts from taking hold in the client's mind. The individual can learn to think of another more positive subject, engage in a pleasant activity, share their feelings, or analyze and reinterpret the thought."[11]

This is why when people get angry, they are encouraged to stop and count to ten—or thirty or one hundred may be an even better idea. It gives you a chance to engage your orbital frontal cortex and think. What are you telling your brain when you pause that way? *It's okay. You have time.* There's a logic to this, of course. If you really did encounter a fight-or-flight situation, you probably *won't* have time to pause. Freezing up is how you die. But when you stop to breathe and think for a minute about what you're feeling, you put your brain into a better connection with your body. You are telling yourself that this is not a situation that requires a survival response.

When you notice anger rising and unhelpful thoughts fueling that anger, thought stopping can be a valuable tool. This technique involves interrupting the cycle of negative thoughts, but it doesn't always have to be a forceful process. The approach can vary, depending on your personality and the situation. Here's how it might look for different individuals:

- **The assertive approach:** When negative thoughts arise, some people find it effective to firmly tell themselves, "Stop!" This can be done internally or even whispered aloud if appropriate.
- **The gentle redirect:** Some people prefer a softer approach, gently guiding their thoughts in a new direction. This may involve quietly saying to yourself, *Let's think about this differently* or *Is there another way to look at this?*
- **The mindful observer:** For those inclined toward mindfulness, you might acknowledge the thought without judgment, saying, *I notice I'm having an angry thought*, and then letting it pass like a cloud in the sky.
- **The visual interrupter:** Visual thinkers might imagine a stop sign, a red light, or even a peaceful scene that can help interrupt the flow of angry thoughts.
- **The physical cue:** Some people find it helpful to pair thought stopping with a physical action, like snapping a rubber band on their wrist or taking a deep breath.
- **The curious questioner:** Instead of commanding yourself to stop,

you might ask, *Is this thought helpful right now?* or *What would be a more constructive way to think about this?*

The key is to find an approach that feels authentic and effective for you. Thought stopping isn't about suppressing emotions or denying reality; it's about creating a pause—a moment of choice between the trigger and your response. This pause allows you to engage your prefrontal cortex, the rational part of your brain, rather than being driven solely by the emotional response from your amygdala.

Remember, the goal is to interrupt the pattern of unhelpful thoughts gently but firmly, creating space for more constructive thinking. With practice, you'll discover which method works best for you in different situations.

Instead of just letting nature run its course, where you just might go on an amygdala-chaperoned journey from mild irritation to provoked frustration to personal indignation to uncontrolled rage, you stop—asking God to give you supernatural power to do so.

Because of the reality of neuroplasticity, it gets a little easier every time you adopt this strategy. Your brain is learning. The neurons are slowly being retrained. The first time will be the hardest and feel the most unnatural. You may need some encouragement and accountability. But the more you do it, the more your brain will learn to do it. And just *wanting* to do it is the first step.

Thought stopping will allow you to have some self-awareness in the moment. As you pause before responding, you can begin to recognize what triggers you. It also gives you a moment to challenge your interpretation of what's going on. Perhaps the way you're perceiving the situation isn't the only way, the right way, the healthy way, or the godly way to view it.

Then what do you do?

You can (prayerfully) think about two important questions.

## Where Is This Anger Coming From?

What is causing me to be offended? Why am I taking this so personally? This is a surprisingly deep question—especially when our level of anger or emotional response feels like it's out of proportion to the situation.

Psychologist Kyle Benson calls this the "anger iceberg."[12] When we see an iceberg in the ocean, much more of it is underneath the water that we cannot see than above the water that we can. Anger is like that. That's why we must be slow to anger, so we can think about what we cannot see.

We may act offended, but in reality, we're anxious. Our anxiety is coming to the surface as irritability. We assume we have an anger problem, but perhaps we truly have an anxiety problem. Why would our anxiety show itself in anger?

Most of the time when we're anxious, it's about something we can't control, like someone's feelings, our circumstances, or what might happen in the future. But there's something about getting angry that makes us feel like we're back in control. It gives us a false sense of power.

Or perhaps rejection is lurking below the surface. It feels more empowering to be offended than to feel rejected. Feeling rejected makes us vulnerable. We don't want to be seen that way, and so instead of dealing with the hurt, we get angry.

When we are offended and get worked up, there is something else going on. What is it? What thought pattern are we caught up in?

It might be *personalization*. This is when we engage in one of our specialties—mind reading. We assume we know another person's intentions and interpret a neutral situation as a personal attack. Or *insecurity* might be our thought pattern that surfaces in times of offense. We're filled with self-doubt. We're supersensitive to perceived slights. Remember when God refused to accept Cain's offering, and instead of responding with humility, Cain reacted by killing his brother? Is it possible Cain was offended and became angry because of insecurity, because Abel's obedience and excellence felt like an indictment on him.

What is lurking underneath our offense can be harder to see, and it's often something we want to keep hidden, so what we show people is . . . anger. Sometimes it's passive. Sometimes it's aggressive. Sometimes it's passive-aggressive.

So we must stop and think, *Where is this anger coming from?*

## What Is It Like for Them?

A second question to ask ourselves when someone offends us is this: *What is it like for them?* It's a question that can help turn our offense into compassion.

In John 4, we find Jesus at a well in the heat of the day. He's hot and thirsty. There's a well right in front of him but he doesn't have anything to draw water from it. That's already enough to make a person irritable. A Samaritan woman approaches the well, and he speaks to her. She's not sure if she should answer. Most Jewish men would be offended if a Samaritan woman were to speak to them.

As their conversation develops, in an effort to get attention off of her, she aims to offend Jesus with a few comments and questions about the proper place of worship, which was a long-standing point of tension between Jews and Samaritans. Jesus doesn't get drawn into her trap of offense. Instead, he reveals himself to her as the living water, the one who can quench her deepest thirst.

When someone's words or actions seem designed to offend us and provoke us, our tendency is to react, to become overly sensitive, to let our level of offense prove our depth of conviction on the issue. But Jesus responds with grace and compassion. How did he do that? I think it's because he knew her and her story. He knew the disappointment she had felt and the betrayal she had experienced. He understood why she would be combative and distrusting toward a man like him. In a world that is quick to think the worst and take offense, choosing compassion is a radical act.

When someone is being offensive, we can respond with compassion. We can think thoughts, not about our hurt, but about *their* hurt. A good question to consider when someone offends us is this: *What is it like for them?*

Look at the person and truly reflect on what it's like for them. When we do that, we'll be more likely to ask questions to better understand them. In my experience, the more curious I am about what someone is dealing with, the more I'll understand what it's like to be them. Instead of feeling offended, we'll feel compassion. Our thoughts aren't focused on ourselves but on them.

In *The 7 Habits of Highly Effective People*, Stephen Covey tells the story of a time he was riding the subway one Sunday morning in New York city. A father boarded the subway with several young children, who immediately began running up and down the aisle, yelling, and throwing things. The father sat with his eyes closed, ignoring or perhaps oblivious to the chaos his children were creating. Covey became increasingly offended. How could this father be so inconsiderate? How could he allow his children to behave so badly? Eventually, unable to contain his anger, Covey turned to the father and said, "Sir, your children are really disturbing a lot of people. I wonder if you couldn't control them a little more?"

The father opened his eyes, looked at what his kids were doing, and then apologized. He explained that they were coming from the hospital where his wife, the kids' mother, had died an hour ago. He said softly, "I don't know what to think, and I guess they don't know how to handle it either." Covey's irritation immediately vanished. His anger gave way to compassion. His offense was replaced with a desire to help.[13] Why?

Because the question he didn't know he should ask was this: *What is it like for them?*

## BREAKING THE PATTERN

I was caught up in thought patterns of offense. The breaking point came on a Tuesday morning. I had spent several hours the previous day responding to critical and cynical emails. I tried to give gentle and pastoral answers, but my patience tank was running out, and my kindness gauge was on empty. And then I opened my email to find a scathing message from a church member I didn't know personally. The words were harsh, critiquing everything from my leadership style to my choice of clothing. I had had enough.

Instead of firing off a rebuttal email, I looked up this fella's phone number and called him directly. I could see my nostrils flaring as my neurotransmitters were firing. I was ready to give him a piece of mind.

The number he saw pop up on his phone just said it was from the church. He didn't know it was me on the other end, giving me the element of surprise. But when a tired, gravelly voice answered, I could tell something was off. "Hello, is this the church?" I was silent for a moment. He asked in a trembling voice, "Are you calling about my son?"

My heart shifted. My thoughts were redirected. "This is Pastor Kyle," I managed to say as my anger began dissipating. "I was calling to talk to you about the email you sent. But first update me on your son."

"He's down in Nashville. The hospital he was taken to after the overdose is telling us he needs to be transferred to an inpatient facility, but we don't know where to send him, and we don't have the money for treatment."

I told him we could help him walk through that, and after talking for a few more minutes, I asked if I could pray for his son. As I prayed over the phone, I could hear him softly crying.

All my self-righteous offense and prideful anger evaporated. Here was a father, terrified by things in his life he couldn't control, lashing out in pain with an email that I had woven into the pattern of offense that was holding my thoughts captive. I had become so focused on my own feelings, so quick to take offense, that I had lost sight of the very reason I became a pastor—to help people through their darkest moments.

## CHAPTER 7

# THE PATTERN OF PLEASURE

## FROM INSTANT GRATIFICATION TO ETERNAL PERSPECTIVE

**M**ichael stares at his reflection in the bathroom mirror, barely recognizing the 372-pound man looking back at him. He has just returned from the doctor's office, where he was weighed for the first time in more than a year.

Michael is forty-two, and his doctor just warned him again about his dangerously high blood pressure and prediabetic condition. It isn't like he hasn't tried. He has been on every diet out there. He subscribes to a calorie-counting app on his phone and has a gym membership, but he can't remember the last time he used either. If you open his kitchen cabinets, you'll find that they are full of child-sized plates he bought to work on portion control, but it's not hard to go back for second and thirds.

Michael's focus has been on behavior modification, but until he understands and addresses how he thinks about food, nothing will change. He thinks it's just that food tastes good and he has a big appetite, but really his thinking about food goes back to a crisp autumn day when an eight-year-old Michael's world shattered. His father, a firefighter, died in the line of duty. The house was filled with somber voices and tear-stained faces. Overwhelmed and confused, Michael retreated to his room, burying his face in a pillow.

A gentle knock on the door. "Mikey?" His mother's voice was thick with emotion. She sat on the edge of his bed, a plate in her hands. "I made your favorite—chocolate chip cookies." The warm, sweet aroma enveloped him as he sat up. His mother pulled him close, and together they ate the cookies in silence. For a brief moment, the weight of loss lifted. The pain in his mind was numbed, just for a minute, by the pleasure of chocolate chips.

At age eight, Michael didn't understand how neurotransmitters work or how the chemical compound of chocolate chips includes phenylethylamine, which can trigger the release of dopamine and theobromine, which would help him feel better. While chocolate in moderation is fine, the equation in Michael's head was clear: The more chocolate he ate, the better he felt.

Whenever Michael felt sad, anxious, or overwhelmed, his mother's response was the same—a batch of fresh cookies and a warm hug. The thought pattern of pleasure was set: *emotional pain → cookies → comfort*.

As Michael grew older, this coping mechanism expanded. Middle school bullies taunting him? A candy bar from the gas station on the way home soothed the sting just a bit. Rejected by the girl he asked to prom? Some ice cream calmed his nerves. Each time life threw a challenge his way, Michael's brain whispered the familiar refrain: "Food will make you feel better." The neural pathway strengthened; the habit deepened.

By college, Michael's weight had become a source of anxiety itself, creating a vicious cycle. Feeling bad about his appearance led to more emotional eating, which led to more weight gain, which led to more eating to feel better.

The years have come and gone, but the thoughts Michael had as an eight-year-old boy still hold him captive and now have all the power of his own brain's neurons to back them up. When he has had a long day at work, a quick stop at the drive-through helps him feel better. When things aren't going well at home, he gets out of the house for some wings and beer. His thought patterns have been reinforced again and again through repeated experiences. It's so deeply ingrained that even as he looks at himself in the mirror, thinking about the unnerving warning of his doctor, he decides he's going to start intermittent fasting tomorrow—but right now what would make him feel better is some chocolate chip cookie dough ice cream.

It feels like the pleasure of eating is what makes life worth living, but in reality, it's what's killing him.

His thought patterns are making him a prisoner of what once was a pleasure. The cookies that once promised comfort from pain have become chains he can't seem to break free from. His thought patterns around food are deeply ingrained, but just as his thinking put him in this prison, changing his thinking can set him free.

I want to pause here for a moment. As I share Michael's story, I'm acutely aware that for some of you, this isn't just a story; it's a mirror reflecting your own struggles, pain, and perhaps shame. I see you. I want you to know that your heart matters deeply to me, and even more so to Jesus.

If Michael's story stirred up feelings of guilt, shame, or hopelessness inside you, please hear me: It's okay. It's okay that this is hard. It's okay if you're fighting back tears or feeling a knot in your stomach. Your pain is valid, and your struggles don't diminish your worth or God's love for you.

Jesus is right there with you in this moment. He's not standing at a distance, shaking his head in disappointment. No, he's right beside you—his heart breaking with yours, his hand reaching out to comfort you. Remember, this is the same Jesus who touched lepers, ate with outcasts, and wept with the brokenhearted. He is not afraid of your pain or your struggles.

## THE UNTHINKABLE

Let's view chocolate chip cookies in Michael's story as a metaphor. Yes, it is possible that chocolate chip cookies are actually chocolate chip cookies.

But they can represent any number of things that promise pleasure but have left us imprisoned.

We'll reflect together on a story from the Old Testament, but before diving in, please know that the following section contains references to sexual assault and violence. This biblical account discusses themes of rape and familial abuse, which some readers, quite understandably, may find distressing. While I believe this raw and honest story can be a source of healing for you, don't hesitate to skip this section and revisit it when you have the support of a trusted friend, counselor, or pastor.

King David's son Amnon and Amnon's half-sister Tamar's story in the Old Testament is one your Sunday school teacher probably didn't teach you. It illustrates how thought patterns are always leading somewhere, and that when left unchecked, thoughts that promise pleasure can lead to devastating decisions.

Amnon's thought pattern began by thinking of something he couldn't have—or, in this case, someone. He wanted to have sex with his half-sister Tamar. (Yeah, oof. And people think the Bible is for prudes?) When that thought first came to his mind, he knew it was a bad idea. But he didn't see any harm in thinking about it; after all, he was never going to act on it. As long as the plan is just happening in his imagination, what's the harm? So he kept thinking about it, but at some point these thoughts started to take him captive. "Amnon became so obsessed with his sister Tamar that he made himself ill" (2 Samuel 13:2). Amnon kept thinking these thoughts until he couldn't *stop* thinking them.

Amnon became consumed with these thoughts. Finally, he told a friend, who hatched a wicked, cruel, and disgusting plan. He suggested that Amnon pretend to be sick, and then when his sister came to his bedroom to check on him, he could seize the opportunity.

No doubt he lustfully played out the scene in his mind numerous times, and then one day, he decided to go for it. A disturbing scene unfolded as she begged him not to do it. She pleaded with him to think about what would happen—how she would be disgraced, and his reputation ruined. "But he refused to listen to her, and since he was stronger than she, he raped her" (2 Samuel 13:14).

It's brutal. Heartbreaking. Wrong. Tamar is devastated.

Amnon thought himself into doing what he once thought unthinkable. A thought that initially promised pleasure brought incredible pain, not only to his life, but to his sister, his whole family, and eventually the entire nation.

Let's think about his thinking here and take a closer look at Amnon's thought pattern. Some of this is speculation, but I'm confident this pattern is reasonably accurate. I see it as a pastor all the time, and as *humans*, we all may well recognize some of these patterns, though thankfully they rarely lead to such serious crimes as the one committed against Tamar. Trace his thoughts:

- **Boundaries crossed:** He begins to think about doing things with her he would never think about doing in real life.
- **Obsession:** His thoughts become more and more constant, and with each thought, he becomes a little more convinced he has to have her.
- **Objectivation:** His obsessive thoughts create a strong neural pathway, where he no longer looks at her as a person but as an object that exists for his pleasure.
- **Entitlement:** As a prince, Amnon is used to getting what he wanted. He often has thoughts like, *I deserve to have what I want*, and *The rules don't apply to me.*
- **Rationalization:** He listens to his friend's plan and probably thinks, *That doesn't sound like that big of a deal*, and *She might want it too.* Maybe in the fantasy of his thoughts, she secretly is wanting him just as much as he wants her.
- **Magnification:** He becomes convinced that his desires have to be satisfied. Besides, he wouldn't have these desires if they aren't intended to be met.
- **Minimization:** As his obsession grows, he thinks only of his pleasure and not of the potential consequences.

When Amnon finally acted on his violent lust, the "pleasure" he dreamed he would experience brought him no satisfaction. It actually delivered the opposite of what he expected. Instead of feelings of satisfaction, he felt contempt. After his encounter with Tamar, "he hated her more than he had loved her" (2 Samuel 13:15). This may sound strange. She didn't do anything to him. Why would he hate her? He was left feeling emptier and more unsatisfied than ever, and my guess is the person he really hated was himself. His immediate hatred of her points to a thought pattern of blame shifting as a way to deal with guilt. He can't look at her without being reminded of what he did and the pain he caused.

Tamar goes and tells her full brother, Absalom, what happened. Absalom is filled with rage but waits for the right moment. He begins having lustful thoughts that are different than his brother's, but just as obsessive. He is going to have his revenge, and he won't be satisfied until he does. Two years later, the right opportunity comes along, and Absalom assassinates Amnon for what he did to Tamar. One prince kills another prince, which actually leads to a civil war.

Amnon's thought patterns didn't develop overnight. They were a gradual corruption of his thinking, each step making the next one easier to justify. The pattern of pleasure—the idea that the pursuit of my happiness should be paramount—is one of the most prevalent and persuasive in our culture. Amnon's story illustrates how the pattern of pleasure progresses in our minds. We can always reverse engineer someone who ruined their life pursuing pleasure with a thought that wasn't taken captive.

## ENTITLED TO PLEASURE

My friend Laurie was an up-and-coming accountant at a large corporation. She began noticing small inefficiencies in the company's financial systems. At first, her thoughts focused on being curious: *I wonder if anyone would notice if I moved a small amount?* That curiosity turned into obsession as she continuously thought about the possibility of taking money and what she would do if she had that kind of cash—like going on Amazon and putting all kinds of things on her wish list. She would fantasize about what it would be like to have enough money to hit the "buy it now" button whenever she wanted.

Those obsessive thoughts led to thoughts of entitlement: *I work harder than everyone else.* Then came the rationalization: *I don't get paid what I deserve.* Then came the minimization: she stopped thinking about the potential consequences and thought only of the payoff.

Eventually, Laurie embezzled well over one hundred thousand dollars. When she was caught, she was not only fired but also arrested. It was devastating to her and her family. It started as a thought that released a little dopamine, but led to her doing something she never thought she was capable of doing.

Scott was in school to become a software engineer. The program was demanding and highly competitive. Scott worked hard, but as a student, he wasn't making much money or landing any promotions. One evening, he decided to place an online bet on the basketball game he was watching. It was a lot more fun watching the game with twenty bucks on the line. His bet hit, and he decided to give online poker a try.

After a long day of classes and homework, it was a great escape. Besides, it wasn't really that bad because he'd never bet more the twenty dollars. But then his cap started to go up. Soon he was betting hundreds of dollars. He fell behind financially, maxing out his credit cards and even taking out student loans to try to win back his losses.

Can you track his thought patterns?

- **Entitlement:** As hard as I work, I deserve to have some fun.
- **Rationalization:** I'm good with numbers, so I have an edge.
- **Magnification:** I won't take big risks, and the upside is I can pay my school bills.

It all began with a thought. A thought that promised pleasure and then delivered anything but.

# THE PLEASURE THOUGHT PATTERN

The truth is that we're all in danger of getting caught up and trapped in the world's pleasure pattern. We need to understand the progression of thoughts because if we don't take these thoughts captive, it's only a matter of time before they take us captive.

### Thought #1: "Doing What Feels Good Will Make Me Happy"

We go after newer, faster, shinier, bigger things because we assume these pleasures will make us happy. We go after circumstances we assume will make us feel good. We go after people, even use people, for the pleasure we think we'll find. We pursue pleasure, hoping to find happiness. Just do it, go after it, get enough of it, and you'll be happy.

But all kinds of studies, not just faith-based studies but also many secular ones, have shown there's no quicker way to be *un*happy than making our lives about happiness. It's sometimes called the "pleasure paradox" or the "happiness illusion." The harder we chase after happiness, the more elusive it becomes. Turns out trying to pursue pleasure makes us miserable.

Joy Davidman, the wife of C. S. Lewis, said, "Living for pleasure is the least pleasurable thing a man can do; if his neighbors don't kill him in disgust, he will slowly die of boredom and powerlessness."[1]

Our culture says happiness is found by pursuing pleasure; God says happiness is found by pursuing him. God wants us to be happy, and this happiness comes from pursuing and knowing him. It's what he tells us in the Bible:

- "Rejoice in the LORD" (Psalm 32:11).
- "Take delight in the LORD" (Psalm 37:4).
- "Worship the LORD with gladness" (Psalm 100:2).
- "Happy are the people whose God is the LORD!" (Psalm 144:15 GNT).
- "Rejoice in the Lord" (Philippians 4:4).

So many people view God as a means to happiness, like it's God's job to provide them with what they need to be happy. No. We don't have God so he can give us blessings to make us happy; *we have God*, and he is the greatest blessing, so he makes us happy.

So we don't pursue pleasure; we pursue God. Happy people don't chase after happiness; they chase after God, and happiness catches them.

### *Thought #2: "I Deserve to Be Happy, Right Now"*

This thought pattern of pleasure is rooted in the thinking that nothing is more important than my immediate happiness. If I think I deserve to be happy or that God's greatest desire is my happiness, then I will be constantly thinking about what makes me happy in the current moment.

This thought is put into our heads thousands of times a day—somewhere between four thousand and ten thousand, to be more exact. That's the number of advertisements the average American is exposed to every day. The dominant theme of those ads is this: "You deserve to be happy, right now." Companies are expected to spend a whopping $389 billion on advertising in the United States in 2024.[2] Which is ironically the estimated cost of buying every person on earth a kazoo, which might make us happy. It's hard to be mad playing a kazoo.

These advertisers know we all want instant happiness, and they understand how our brains work. Neuroscientists have found that the promise of getting something we don't have stimulates the prefrontal cortex and activates the limbic system, which is the emotional part of our brain. So they want you to feel like you are missing something that will make you happy, but that feeling is the opposite of happiness; it's discontent.

If our lives are dominated by the thought, *I deserve to be happy*, then we will believe immediate pleasure is the path we should take. We'll think that whatever makes us happy must be right, and that whatever makes us unhappy must be wrong. Which means that a lot of what we think is right will be wrong, and a lot of what we think is wrong will be right.

Consider this list of things that *don't* make us immediately happy but *are* in our best interest:

- **Waking up early:** Immediate effect: hating life and everyone in it for the first hour. Long-term benefit: feeling like you've completed a day's work before you've had breakfast.
- **Exercise:** Immediate effect: sweating like a pig and questioning your life choices. Long-term benefit: looking good naked—oh, and living longer.
- **Saving money:** Immediate effect: saying goodbye to your social life and hello to ramen noodles. Long-term benefit: being able to take care of yourself and give to others.
- **Difficult conversations:** Immediate effect: wishing you could fake your own death to avoid the awkwardness. Long-term benefit: having peace and boundaries instead of moving to another state to avoid running into the person.
- **Home maintenance:** Immediate effect: spending your day off trying not to cuss while googling "What does water damage smell like?" Long-term benefit: living in a house that's nice to come home to.

If you are a Christian living in the Western world, chances are that at some point along the way, the cultural thought of *I deserve to be happy* morphs into an even more dangerous thought: *It's God's job to make me happy.* This thought will almost certainly lead to your feeling *un*happy with God. Eventually, you'll think, *I tried the God thing, but . . .*

*I still have cancer.*
*My kids are still a mess.*
*I'm not better off financially.*
*The divorce still happened.*
*We still haven't got pregnant.*
*I'm still single.*
*I'm not happier.*

If we think that immediate pleasure and happiness is what God wants most for our lives, then we'll start to believe discomfort, delay, or incon-venience is God's fault. If something isn't going right, we'll blame him for not doing his job.

### Thought #3: "Pleasure Is Determined by My Immediate Circumstances"

I'll admit it. I can be a bit of a diva when I fly. I expect a certain level of comfort and convenience. I've become a "preferred partner," which comes with some benefits such as boarding early—although I don't know why being on a plane longer is considered a benefit. Occasionally, I even get bumped up to first class.

One of the first times I flew in first class I found myself sitting in the window seat next to a guy who complained about *everything*. He complained about the boarding process, the temperature, the light com-ing through the window that was getting in his eyes. I was next to the window and had planned on closing the window shade, but not anymore; now it's staying open the whole flight. *I'll give you something to complain about, mister.*

He continued to complain, so I finally said, "Well . . . but . . . we are really fortunate to be in first class." He scoffed and said, "Oh, you won't find me flying coach." Then he added, "The derriere of passengers has grown an average of fifteen inches since this plane was built." Except he didn't say derriere.

I gave him a sort of awkward laugh, and he said, "No, seriously. Look it up. The derrieres of passengers have grown an average of fifteen inches."

I looked it up.

He was telling the truth.

This man felt so entitled that he had angrily researched the derriere sizes of passengers on airplanes and had documented his research! He couldn't imagine sitting in coach, where the seats were built for derrieres fifteen inches smaller.

As I got off the plane, I wanted to make sure the flight attendant knew I wasn't friends with this guy, so I told her, "Hey, I'm sorry about that guy.

You'd think he'd be glad just to be sitting in first class." She said, "Oh, we expect that in first class. The most unhappy fliers are always in first class."

As I walked out, I was struck by the irony. People in coach think, *If I was just in first class, if I just had more space, if I could just get my drinks a bit earlier, if it wasn't so crammed back here, if it was more like it is up there,* then *I would be happy.* But that's not how it works. Abundance doesn't lead to pleasure; instead, it often leads to entitlement, discontent, and complaining.

*Happiness* comes from the same root word as *happen,* and the happiness we believe in depends on what's happening to us and around us.

The thoughts we think about pleasure have a repeating refrain: *I'd be happy if only . . .*

> *I had a new house.*
> *I had a nicer car.*
> *I had a better spouse.*
> *I had a different job.*
> *I lived in a different city.*
> *I went to a different school.*
> *I had a great body.*

If those things brought pleasure, then Americans should be the happiest people on the planet, because we have the best circumstances in the history of the world. But a Gallup Poll ranked the United States as twenty-third in the world on the happiness scale.[3]

Another study revealed that as our circumstances in America continue to improve (more comfort, more convenience, more money, more entertainment), depression, low self-esteem, hopelessness, and suicide have continued to rise.[4] In fact, some studies show that valuing happiness may diminish happiness.[5]

You may understand all of this because your circumstances *did* change, yet it *didn't* make you happier. You thought, *If only I could make this much money, I'd be happy,* but you now make that much money and . . .

the new amount needed for happiness has changed. When that day comes, you still won't be happier. The amount will just change again. It's always changing, and it's never less.

The apostle Paul often faced circumstances that were anything but pleasurable. Just for being a Christian, he was attacked, beaten, thrown in jail, and left for dead. How did he respond? He wrote these words from a dark, dank prison cell:

> I have learned to be content whatever the circumstances. I know what it is to be in need, and I know what it is to have plenty. I have learned the secret of being content in any and every situation, whether well fed or hungry, whether living in plenty or in want. I can do all this through him who gives me strength.
>
> **PHILIPPIANS 4:11–13**

In that same letter, Paul writes, "Rejoice in the Lord always" (Philippians 4:4).

This is someone who has made his thoughts obedient to Christ. There was no pleasure to be found in his circumstances, but he had learned (verse 11) to find his satisfaction in his relationship with Jesus. *Learned* implies that this way of thinking wasn't something that came natural to him; it was a process of training himself to think differently about challenges and struggles.

### Thought #4: "I'll Have Pleasure When I Get What I Don't Have"

We think pleasure is found in getting what we don't have or getting what *they've* got. We're usually thinking not about what we already have, but rather about what we want. Instead, the Bible teaches us to take pleasure in what we already have. First Thessalonians 5:16–18 reads, "Rejoice always, pray continually, give thanks in all circumstances." We're not told to be thankful *for* all circumstances, but we can be thankful *in* all circumstances. Intentional thankfulness and gratitude shape our brains so that we stop noticing what is missing and start being more aware of what we have been given.

Choosing gratitude is how you take unhappy thoughts captive.

The National Institutes of Health conducted a study confirming that people who showed more gratitude overall had higher levels of activity in the hypothalamus.[6] (I know, *hypo-what-a-mus?* Still with the big words, Kyle?) The hypothalamus is the part of the brain that controls bodily functions like eating Funyuns, drinking kombucha, and getting a good night's sleep. So the research has essentially demonstrated that gratitude has a positive impact on everything else we do with our bodies.

Choosing gratitude has also been shown to make us happy. Expressing gratitude caused subjects to experience an increase in dopamine hits, the reward neurotransmitter that makes the brain happy. In short, each time a subject expressed gratitude, the brain said, "Ooh! Do it again!" In this way, feeling gratitude led to feeling more gratitude, which led to feeling more and more gratitude still. "Once you start seeing things to be grateful for, your brain starts looking for more things to be grateful for. That's how the virtuous cycle gets created."[7]

Since that's all true, why don't you wrestle down any thoughts that tell you pleasure will be found when you get what you don't have, and instead choose to be grateful for what you do have now?

A study done by psychologists Robert Emmons and Michael McCullough has shed light on just how impactful grateful thoughts can be. In their 2003 research, published in the *Journal of Personality and Social Psychology*, they set out to measure the effects of grateful thoughts verses thoughts of discontentment.[8]

The researchers divided participants into three groups. One group was asked to write weekly about things they were grateful for, another about daily irritations, and a third about neutral events. This journaling continued for ten weeks, with the researchers measuring various aspects of the participants' well-being throughout the study.

The results were remarkable.

Those who focused on gratitude reported feeling better about their lives as a whole and were more optimistic about the future. It's as if the simple act of acknowledging the good in their lives painted their entire worldview with a brighter brush.

But the benefits didn't stop at mental well-being. Surprisingly, the gratitude group also reported fewer physical complaints and spent more time exercising compared to the other groups. It seems that thinking thankful thoughts also lead to a healthier body.

What was especially interesting is that those practicing grateful thinking were more likely to report having helped someone with a personal problem. Gratitude, it appears, doesn't just make us feel better—it makes people around us feel better.

The pattern of this world tells us pleasure will come when we get more, while gratitude teaches us to take pleasure in what we already have.

A. J. Jacobs, in his book titled *Thanks a Thousand*, tells of his quest to express gratitude to all the different people involved in making his morning cup of coffee possible. When he began to realize he needed more gratitude in his life, he began a ritual of a premeal prayer that thanked the people who helped provide for his daily needs, like the farmer, trucker, and cashier. One day, his son challenged him to thank them in person. Jacobs took this challenge to heart, picked his specific item to be thankful for (the one he said he can't live without), and embarked on a global mission— Project Gratitude, he called it—to personally thank a multitude of people involved in the coffee industry.[9]

His journey highlighted the intricate web of contributions from people all over the world, from baristas to farmers, road pavers, and even the inventor of his coffee cup lid. His project taught him to look up and acknowledge people, savor moments, recognize hidden masterpieces in ordinary objects, and understand that gratitude can lead to genuine feelings of thankfulness. He learned to focus on the thousands of things that go right in a day instead of the few that go wrong.

Through this extensive gratitude practice, Jacobs experienced a shift in perspective, realizing the world's interconnectedness and the importance of appreciating the small details. He concluded that gratitude could spark further positive actions, inspiring him to support causes like safe water access. Jacobs encourages all of us to follow our own gratitude trails, whether big or small, to transform our outlook on life. It will deepen our gratitude for the simple pleasures. And the more we do it, the more we'll find ourselves doing it. So why not start now? You can begin by keeping a gratitude journal or downloading a gratitude app as you set out on your quest to stop paying attention to what you don't have and start being grateful for what you do have.

It's time to stop being held captive by our thoughts and start taking our thoughts captive. Like Michael, Amnon, Laurie, and Scott, our thought pattern can make us a prisoner of pleasure. What promises comfort will become chains from which we can't break free. Our thinking may have put us in prison, but changing our thinking can set us free.

## CHAPTER 8

# THE PATTERN OF DESPAIR

## FROM DISTORTED THINKING TO DELIVERANCE

Overwhelmed with despair, Martin Luther King Jr. sat alone late one night at his kitchen table, questioning whether he could go on. Typically buoyant, full of hope, King felt like he was drowning, despondent, and hopeless.

It was January 1956. Following the Montgomery bus boycott—sparked by the arrest of Rosa Parks—King was facing intense resistance and hostility from local authorities and White supremacists, including threats against his life and family. He was committed to the civil rights movement but had decided he could no longer lead it.[1]

# THE PATTERN OF DESPAIR

My guess is you've been there. You know what it's like to cower from your fears at the kitchen table. You know the feeling of hope evaporating. You've stared at the ceiling in the middle of the night and had your thoughts spiral from anxious notions into worst-case scenario predictions of impending, unavoidable doom. What started out as, "It's time to go nighty night; I'm going to get warm under the covers and get a great night's sleep!" somehow turns into tossing and turning in a bed of despair.

Here's some morbid (but in another sense good) news: You are not alone.

- Since 1990, there has been a rise in self-reported unhappiness.[2]
- Over the last decades, "diseases of despair"—such as substance abuse, alcohol dependence, and suicidal thoughts—have soared.[3]
- Since 1999, there has been a dramatic increase in "deaths by despair"—defined as deaths by suicide, drug and alcohol poisoning, and alcoholic liver disease and cirrhosis.[4]
- Rates of depression in the United States have reached record highs.[5]
- Experts call our time the "age of anxiety" with anxiety disorders now ranking as the most common mental illness in America, affecting more than 40 million adults—19.1 percent of the population.[6]

There's a way of thinking that invariably weaves a pattern that leads to despair. It starts with *distorted thinking*. We view an event or situation in an inaccurate way that puts it in a negative light. We may overgeneralize (draw broadly pessimistic conclusions from limited evidence), personalize (unfairly attribute something bad that happened to a personal flaw), or catastrophize (assume the worst will happen).

After distorted thinking comes *discouragement*. We begin to dwell on the negative thoughts without seeking a solution or positive way to look at it. We judge and blame ourselves, which causes us to lose confidence and enthusiasm.

Discouragement leads to *disillusionment*. As we spiral, we wonder if our expectations have been unrealistic and start to lose faith that things can be different or get better. We wonder if our efforts are futile. And if they are, well, what about life itself?

Disillusionment ushers us into *despair*. If any of us have ever been there, we know this is not a place we want to be. We feel like there is no solution or improvement possible and move into a state of resignation, helplessness, and hopelessness. We might feel trapped in our situation and come to the (false) conclusion that there's no way out.

This is bleak. I hope you don't relate to any of it, but perhaps you do. At some point, and to some degree, most of us will. When we find ourselves caught up in thought patterns of despair, what do we do? Can we renew our minds in a way that we become transformed rather than conformed? How do we invite God into our despair?

Well, as I said earlier, *you are not alone*. I know what it's like to find myself in this pattern of thinking, lying awake in the night, and wondering if things are going to be okay. And what's more, one of the greatest men of all time—a man after God's own heart—knows what it's like as well.

Many of the psalms in the Bible were written by Israel's King David. Some of them are masterpieces of celebration and praise, but others, well, aren't. They go to the depths and into the darkness. They communicate despair with honesty.

Let's take a moment to walk through Psalm 55 because it's an amazing example of how David does this very intentionally. David makes six shifts in his thinking—thought shifts we can make as well.

If you haven't read Psalm 55 for a while, take a moment and read it twice, letting it sink in and trying to remember a time when you felt what David is expressing. Then before we walk through the shifts in thinking, take a few minutes to identify which one you may be struggling with now—or which one you gravitate toward in stressful times:

- distorted thinking
- discouragement
- disillusionment
- despair

_____

_____

_____

_____

_____

_____

_____

_____

_____

_____

_____

_____

_____

## SHIFT ONE: FROM SELF-CONFIDENCE TO CRYING OUT

One day, I noticed that our master bathroom's carpet needed to be replaced. I thought, *I think it'd be better if we made the bathroom floor tile instead of carpet. I can do that. I will tile the master bathroom floor.*

When the next Saturday morning came, I told my wife, "Hey, I'm gonna tile the master bathroom floor."

She looked at me with the same look she gave our toddler son when he said he was going to be Spiderman one day. When she saw I was serious, she pointed her finger at me and started laughing. The pointed finger may not have been literal, but her laugh implied a pointed finger.

This only made me more determined. My thought was, *I got this. I can do anything I set my mind to.*

I went to Home Depot and sat through their forty-five-minute class on tiling a floor. My thoughts of determination were reinforced by thoughts of confidence, but I'll admit that, for the first time, I thought, *Maybe carpet in the bathroom would be more comfortable.*

I went home with all the supplies, tore out the carpet, threw it away, and came back to the bathroom.

Do you know what was underneath the carpet?

Plywood!

I'm not sure what I was expecting, but the plywood scared me.

I looked at the plywood and thought, *What have I done? I cannot tile a bathroom floor. I don't got this. I need help.* I had quickly progressed from distorted thinking to disillusionment to discouragement.

What did I do?

We didn't have the money to pay a professional, so for the next month we had a master bathroom with a plywood floor. Instead of admitting that I may have gotten in over my head, I tried to convince my wife that the plywood floor was decorative and "old-world trendy." I didn't want to ruin the aesthetic by putting modern tile on something so beautiful.

She never bought it.

Finally, in my despair, I did what I should have done from the beginning. I humbled myself and asked a friend who enjoys home improvement projects for his help. He came over, and we knocked it out in an afternoon.

We all like to think with determination, *I got this. I don't need help.*

And then when something goes wrong, our thoughts of determination can turn into thoughts of discouragement. We can go from independent to *more* independent. Like, *God isn't doing anything. He isn't coming through for me. It looks like I'm on my own. I guess I have to put my hope in myself. If I don't fix this, no one will.* But we need to be humble enough to admit, *I don't have this. I need to cry out for help.*

David did that. Check out how he begins his psalm:

> Listen to my prayer, O God.
> Do not ignore my cry for help!
> Please listen and answer me,
> for I am overwhelmed by my troubles.
>
> PSALM 55:1–2 NLT

This doesn't sound like same confident David who marched out and started talking trash to the giant Goliath. He didn't seem overwhelmed by his troubles in that moment. But the years have passed, and David finds himself at the kitchen table, awake in the middle of the night, and he openly admits he's overwhelmed by his troubles. He cries out to God.

You may have grown up learning that feeling anxious or afraid was not okay. Perhaps you had a parent who taught you that expressing feelings was weak. Or maybe you grew up in a church that made it seem like emotions weren't spiritual and weakness revealed a lack of faith.

No.

David is vulnerable in his prayer to God. He tells God he's not competent and cries out for help.

I wonder if that was especially hard for David because he had a certain reputation. He was known for having no fear. After taking out Goliath, it would have been tempting to never be vulnerable enough to admit having thoughts of despair.

Admitting our needs takes a lot of courage. But there is no weakness in feeling overwhelmed. There is no shame in feeling stressed out.

When we find our thoughts moving from discouragement to desperation, we can cry out and be honest with God, just like David did.

*I am overwhelmed by my troubles.*

*I can't do this anymore. This burden is too heavy to carry.*

*I'm not brave enough, not wise enough, not strong enough.*

One of the most dangerous thoughts we can have is this: *I got this. I don't need help.* The courageous thing, the strong thing, is to say, *God, help. I'm overwhelmed. Do not ignore my cry. Rescue me.* It's not strong or courageous to go through life pretending we feel a certain way when we really don't.

The first shift in our thinking is from self-confidence to crying out.

## SHIFT TWO: FROM GENERIC TO SPECIFIC

What is David crying out about? Well, we don't know. He hasn't said.

But as he continues to pray, watch how he shifts from generic to specific:

My enemies shout at me,

    making loud and wicked threats.

They bring trouble on me

    and angrily hunt me down.


My heart pounds in my chest.

    The terror of death assaults me.

Fear and trembling overwhelm me,

    and I can't stop shaking.

PSALM 55:3–5 NLT


*Now* we know. David is specific about what is stressing him out and causing his despair—he has enemies hunting him down and threatening death.

David goes on to tell God about a friend who betrayed him:

As for my companion, he betrayed his friends;

    he broke his promises.

His words are as smooth as butter,

    but in his heart is war.

His words are as soothing as lotion,

    but underneath are daggers!

PSALM 55:20–21 NLT


See how David makes a shift from the generic to the specific as he prays?

When our thought patterns are generic, we feel overwhelmed by the broad and undefined fears threatening us. When we think more specifically, it gives us perspective and keeps our desperation in check.

Have you ever felt ensnared in the pattern of despair when thinking about money? You have bills to pay, debt that's adding up, and nothing in savings. When we think generically about our money problems, the situation feels impossible and desperate. This is why Dave Ramsey and other financial gurus recommend a series of "baby steps" to get on top of our money. By shifting our thoughts from generic to specific, it's not as overwhelming and what we need to do next feels more doable. We make progress on what felt impossible by simply looking at the next step.

When we feel desperate, we may find ourselves praying generically, but we need to pray *specifically*. That's exactly what God invites us to do: "Cast all your anxiety on him because he cares for you" (1 Peter 5:7).

God cares about us and invites us to specifically bring to him whatever is causing our despair. There is power in naming that, because this process can actually have a measurable effect on our brains and emotional state. Neuroscientific research has shown that putting feelings into words—a process called "affect labeling"—can help regulate our emotional experiences. And it's part of what happens when we cast our anxieties on the Lord in prayer.

This process of naming or labeling our feelings can activate the prefrontal cortex, which is involved in emotional regulation, while simultaneously reducing activity in the amygdala. In essence, by naming our anxieties, we can shift our brain activity from emotional centers to areas associated with thinking and language.

A 2007 study led by UCLA psychologist Matthew Lieberman found that verbalizing our feelings makes our sadness, anger, and pain less intense.[7] This suggests that when we pray specifically about our anxieties, naming them to God, we're not just performing a spiritual exercise; we're also engaging in a practice that has been scientifically shown to help manage our emotions.

So when God invites us to cast our anxieties on him, he is not just offering spiritual comfort; he is inviting us into a practice that aligns with the way he designed our brains to function. By specifically naming our concerns in prayer, we're taking these thoughts captive and partnering with God in the process of emotional regulation and healing.

We're thinking about our thoughts, and here's an amazing one: If it's on our minds, it's on God's heart.

Here is another invitation from God:

Do not be anxious about anything, but in every situation, by prayer and petition, with thanksgiving, present your requests to God. And the peace of God, which transcends all understanding, will guard your hearts and your minds in Christ Jesus.

PHILIPPIANS 4:6–7

How do you move from panic to peace? You take every thought captive and turn each worry into a prayer.

If you're worried about your marriage, pray about it.

If you're worried about a decision you have to make, pray about it.

If you're worried about whether you'll be able to pay rent, pray about it. Specifically.

You can, because if it's on your mind, it's on God's heart.

I want to acknowledge something important. I know that for some of you, especially those who are grappling with deep-seated feelings of anxiety and despair, Paul's words in Philippians and my words on this page may feel frustratingly simplistic. They may even come across as indifferent to the real and complex challenges you're facing. I get it. The last thing I want to do is minimize your struggles or suggest that there's an easy fix-it button. But too often prayer is a tool that doesn't get used. I don't want this to sound dismissive of your despair, but in your despair, don't be dismissive of the power of prayer.

Sometimes we pray too generically: *God, I'm feeling really anxious.*

I wonder if that just makes us more anxious. We become anxious about our anxiety.

I feel overwhelmed, and then I start feeling overwhelmed about feeling overwhelmed!

So, what would happen if we followed David's example and prayed specifically?

If we identified our negative thinking, then captured and challenged those negative thoughts by bringing them to God in prayer?

This powerful strategy is not only found in the Bible; it has been confirmed by science. One study investigated the effectiveness of cognitive restructuring techniques to deal with depression. Cognitive restructuring is the process of identifying and challenging negative thoughts—in other words, taking our thoughts captive. In this study, participants who received cognitive therapy showed reduced activation in brain regions associated with negative emotional processing.[8] Another study found that cognitive bias modification programs—therapy aimed at helping participants develop positive interpretations of their circumstances—can lead to reductions in anxiety.[9] This is modern psychology catching up with what David knew in his bones.

Therapists will do this with us, and for many of us it will be a great step to take, but we can also do this with God. We can identify our issues and pray specifically about them.

In David's case, there was a person in his life who had him feeling overwhelmed. We're not told his name, but clearly David had someone specific in mind. (If you know David's insane *Game of Thrones*–style biography, you might have some ideas.)

Maybe for you it's a person too. So, what is it about this person that creates anxiety for you? Pray specifically. Perhaps you have a friend who has ghosted you. You don't understand. Pray about it. It may be a person you wish would feel a certain way about you. You want them to have feelings they don't have, and it's stressing you out. You have "what if" questions: *What if she never feels that way? What if he never says it? What if he never asks? What if she cheats?* Pray about it.

It might be your child. If only you could just *control* your kid—their decisions, their friendships, their life choices. But there's so much we can't control, and we have other "what if" questions: *What if they can't come back from this one? What if they don't turn things around? What if they marry the person they're dating? What if they never come back home? What if they never leave home?* Pray about it.

Specifically.

It's how we take our thoughts captive.

# SHIFT THREE: FROM MY WAY TO GOD'S WAY

David is telling God why he's feeling desperate.

He also tells God what he wants to do, how he'd like to deal with these lousy feelings:

> Oh, that I had wings like a dove;
>> then I would fly away and rest!
> I would fly far away
>> to the quiet of the wilderness.
> How quickly I would escape—
>> far from this wild storm of hatred.
>
> PSALM 55:6–8 NLT

I've felt that way. *I just want to get out of here.*

You probably have too. You can relate to David's train of thought. He has problems, stress, and anxiety, and he just wants to run. *But* he knows his way is not the right way. There is a right way to deal with our feelings, and running isn't it.

To deal with our feelings in the right way, we first have to notice them. That comes easy for some, but not all of us. I wasn't taught to feel my feelings. Being stoic seemed more spiritual. I knew I was supposed to be joyful always, and feelings like sadness seemed incompatible with joy. Did that mean I never felt sad? No, it just meant I did everything I could to suppress any "bad" feelings. It took me a long time to understand that you can be joyful and have sorrow at the same time, and that with God's help, sorrow can be turned into joy—but it can't be done by denying the sadness.

That might be obvious to you, but it was hard-fought wisdom for me.

You can't pretend-your-problems-don't-exist your way into joy. You must feel your feelings and *think* about your feelings. We can't run from them. You pick them up, and you run with them to God. The right way is to invite God into it. That's what David does:

> But I will call on God,
>> and the LORD will rescue me.
> Morning, noon, and night
>> I cry out in my distress,
>> and the LORD hears my voice.

**PSALM 55:16–17 NLT**

David names his despair and then invites God *into* it, as if to say, *God, my way is to run away, but I'm calling on you instead. I want to do this your way. I want to run to you.*

I wonder what *your* way is of dealing with despair. It might be to run. Or fight. Or double down with a determination to overcome when you're feeling overwhelmed. Is it healthy? Is it unhealthy? Whatever it is, *you can invite God into it.* You are not alone.

## SHIFT FOUR: FROM INTERMITTENT TO CONSISTENT

Perhaps the only time you've ever thought of the word *intermittent* is with windshield wipers. You're driving along with your windshield wipers set to intermittent, and suddenly you jump when they pop up in front of you. *Oh, I forgot I had them on!* Because when something is intermittent, it just happens once in a while.

On the other hand, consistent is predictable and constant.

I urge you to pray when you're feeling desperate. You may be thinking, *I already do. That's when I pray—when I'm feeling desperate.*

We tend to pray about things when we're feeling desperate. We follow the example of that great theologian Jelly Roll: "I only talk to God when I need a favor. And I only pray when I ain't got a prayer."[10]

I think part of the reason we pray so intermittently has to with what we focus our minds on—remember the law of cognition and the rule of exposure from section 1? A lot of us, from our first waking thoughts, focus not on God but on our anxiety. How?

We wake up, pick up our phones, and read the news or check work emails. Then we look at our calendar and to-do list and take note of all the things we have to get done today. So in the first twenty minutes of our day, we're reminded of everything that's wrong in the world, of all those things in life that put pressure on us. We start our days by focusing on our anxiety.

At night, we watch TV, get in bed, and keep scrolling through our social media apps. We end our day by reminding ourselves that everyone else's lives are filled with love and laughter. But it doesn't feel like our lives are.

*Why am I the only who feels this way?*
*Why is everyone else's house so nicely decorated?*
*Why is no one else overweight?*

And we fall asleep focusing on our anxiety.

But look again at what David wrote:

> But I will call on God,
> > and the LORD will rescue me.
> Morning, noon, and night
> > I cry out in my distress,
> > and the LORD hears my voice.

**PSALM 55:16–17 NLT**

David's take: "My strategy for dealing with distress and combatting the despairing thoughts is praying morning, noon, and night."

I love that.

He takes his thoughts captive. *I'm focused on God. That's how I start and end my day. And that's where I am in between. That was yesterday, and today. That will be tomorrow. My thoughts are God-directed, prayerful thoughts.*

My strong encouragement is to pray both when you are feeling desperate *and* when you're not feeling desperate.

What if you were to take David's advice and commit to focusing on God morning, noon, and night?

What if you were to wake up, pick up your Bible, and read a chapter so that in the first minutes of your day you would be reminded of the truth of God you want to live by.

What if, like David, you were to take a few minutes at noon to recenter yourself, to call on God, to refocus your thoughts?

What if at night you were to end your day by praying and reminding yourself of things you are grateful for, things that fill your life with love and laughter?

Do you think this strategy might help alleviate some anxiety? Might it drown out some of your despair instead of you drowning in it? I bet it would.

## SHIFT FIVE: FROM TALKING TO GOD ABOUT HIMSELF TO TALKING TO HIMSELF ABOUT GOD

David starts off being honest with God about his despair. Then—and this is huge—he begins to be honest with himself about who God is. He stops talking to God about his despair and starts talking to his despair about God.

David reminds himself who God is, what God has done, and what God will do.

> He ransoms me and keeps me safe
>> from the battle waged against me,
>> though many still oppose me.
> God, who has ruled forever,
>> will hear me and humble them.
>
> **PSALM 55:18-19 NLT**

The way we overcome negative thinking, strongholds, and the world's mold is to capture our thoughts and make them obedient to Christ.

That's what David does here. He captures his despairing thoughts and renews his mind by telling himself truths about God. That's what I hope we'll learn to do as well.

If we're not careful, we can pray in a way that makes us even more anxious. If we just give God a list of all of our concerns, we only remind ourselves of everything that's wrong.

One of the thought patterns that leads to despair is called *rumination*, which is characterized by repetitive, consistent, negative thinking. We often see some common themes:

- past mistakes
- embarrassing moments
- unresolved conflict
- worries about the future
- depression symptoms

When we ruminate, we focus on distressing thoughts. We think about problems over and over. This is understandable, of course, but there's a problem. Rumination is *not* an effective strategy for dealing with thoughts of despair. Imagine watching a movie, only to have it take a turn you don't like. A scene is upsetting, and you wish it was different. So, what do you do? You watch that scene again and then rewind it and watch it again and then rewind it and watch it again. Each time you watch, it you're hoping for a different ending. But you know that won't be the case, and that's rumination.

While David starts his prayer with ruminating thoughts, he shifts to taking his anxious thoughts captive. He goes from talking to God about himself to talking to himself about God. He's like, *Hey, buddy, don't you remember who God is? Yeah, you do. You remember what he's done. This situation is not too hard for him. You might be overwhelmed, but he's not. He's got this. He's got you. You don't need to worry.*

The principle here is simple—it's one of attention. Where we put our focus will determine how safe we are feeling. If someone walking on a tightrope focuses on the hard ground far below them, how will they feel? But if they focus on the rope—how strong it is, how resilient, how trustworthy and tested—well, wouldn't that be a different story?

Do you ever remind yourself who God is, what God has done, and what God will do? If not, gently ask yourself why. Think of something you love. Music? The beauty and form of it are from God. Nature? Not a flower blooms without his knowledge, and every mountain rose at his command. A child? Their very *bones* were formed in the womb at his quiet command. You are his. All things are his.

That's what you can do with stress. You talk to God, and then you talk to yourself about God. *He's got this. He's got me. I don't need to worry.*

And this will lead you to the last shift.

## SHIFT SIX: FROM WORRY TO WORSHIP

David begins in a state of distress because he has enemies lining up against him. He is overwhelmed. But he prays honestly and specifically. He asks God to jump into the driver's seat. Morning, noon, and night, he reminds himself who God is and what God has done.

And what happens? He goes from worrying to worshiping.

The psalms are actually songs, prayers set to music and sung aloud. David is singing these words.

He starts out in Psalm 55 with these words: "Do not ignore my cry for help! I am overwhelmed by my troubles."

Look how he ends:

> Give your burdens to the LORD,
> and he will take care of you.
>
> **PSALM 55:22 NLT**

David isn't worried anymore; he is worshiping. As he prays, he is reminded of who God is, and he can't help but praise God. As he does, his worship drowns out his worry.

I'm not sure worship and worry can coexist. It doesn't mean the problems go away, that the anxiety goes away. But it loses much of its power over us. The pattern of desperation gives way to the pattern of dependence.

David counsels us, "Give your burdens to the LORD, and he will take care of you." You can trust him. It's not, "Give your burdens to the LORD, and he will solve all of your problems." Trust God. Remember who he is and what he has done, and your worry will turn into worship.

## I HEARD THE VOICE

At the beginning of the chapter, we saw Martin Luther King Jr. sitting at his table, completely despondent and feeling ready to quit because of the resistance he faced and the death threats aimed at him.

What would you do in that moment?

He prayed.

King sat in the silence, overwhelmed by his troubles. He cried out to God, and God answered. King describes feeling God's presence with him there in the kitchen and then hearing an inner voice encouraging him to persevere: "I heard the voice of Jesus saying still to fight on. He promised never to leave me, never to leave me alone. No, never alone. No, never alone. He promised never to leave me, never to leave me alone."[11] King went from worry to worship as he spoke words from an old hymn called "Never Alone."[12]

His encounter with Jesus renewed his resolve in the righteousness of the civil rights cause and led him to keep fighting the fight. He took his thoughts captive, and with God's help, he defeated the pattern of despair.

You can do the same at your own kitchen table.

# SECTION 3

# TRANSFORMED THINKING

## *... but be transformed by the renewing of your minds*

**n the previous sections,** we've explored the power of our thoughts and the patterns of this world that so often shape our thinking. We've seen how easily our minds can be conformed to ways of thinking that lead us away from God's best for us. But God doesn't leave us there. He offers us a way out, a path to transformation.

The apostle Paul writes in Romans 12:2, "Do not conform to the pattern of this world, but be transformed by the renewing of your mind." This transformation isn't just a nice idea or a spiritual metaphor; it's a practical reality that we can experience in our daily lives.

In this section, we'll explore what it means to have our minds renewed and how we can actively participate in this transformative process. As you read the upcoming chapters, remember that these aren't merely spiritual exercises; they're powerful tools that align with the way God designed our brains to function. As we practice these principles, we'll see how they reshape our neural pathways, leading to lasting change in our thoughts, emotions, and behaviors.

This transformation isn't so much about having more willpower or trying harder as it is about practices that help us surrender our minds to God and allow his truth to reshape our thinking. It's a journey of cooperation with the Holy Spirit, who empowers us to think in new ways.

## CHAPTER 9

# THE SPECIAL OPS OF THE MIND

## FROM REACTIVE THOUGHTS TO STRATEGIC VICTORY

How would you like an opportunity to train with one of the most elite fighting forces in the modern world?

I was invited by text to do just that. My friend, who has connections at a military base nearby, was reaching out to me. I can't tell you where, what elite force, or what the mission was—top secret info, you understand. Highly classified. As a matter of fact, *I've probably already said too much.*

About a half dozen of my buddies were going to be a part of this exercise. We were civilians, but in our minds, we formed a superior, specially chosen unit coming together to help our special forces train for, you know, world-saving stuff. I figured my part in the training exercise wouldn't be too physically demanding. I'd stand on the sidelines, like at a football game, and make some brilliant observations for the good of national security.

As the time grew closer, I began to hear stories that indicated the experience might be a little more hands-on than I expected. We'd be playing the part of enemy combatants. When the special forces team attacked, my group would fight back and drive them out. The six of us began to text back and forth, talking a little trash, boasting about our personal exploits of valor and courage.

At some point, I noticed we were using a lot of emojis in our text stream, which was a little disconcerting. As a rule, if your emoji game is on point, you're less likely to do well against special forces. When we arrived at the military base, we signed waiver after waiver—which, all by itself, pointed toward dismemberment or even death. At that point, as my research would tell me, my hypothalamus had begun to leak decent amounts of cortisol and norepinephrine into my system. In other words, my courage was replaced by *stress*.

None of us spoke it aloud, but we all had a look that said, *What have I gotten myself into?*

We geared up, meaning we were about to face arguably the most elite group of warriors in the modern world, wearing skateboard pads and armed with paintball guns.

We rode in the back of a pickup truck to what looked like a Third-World village after heavy conflict. As we got out of the truck, one of the men said, "I really think we can win this thing, guys." But his voice cracked, up into Mickey Mouse range, as he said it. The message I heard was, *We're in big trouble. Let's keep our eyes peeled for a good place to hide.*

We were then separated and directed to go into different houses, where we were instructed to wait for the special forces team to show up so we could engage them.

As I stared through a broken window into the darkness of night, I was very much aware that I had no idea what I was doing. Suddenly, out of nowhere, a half dozen Chinook and Blackhawk helicopters flew in without lights. Dozens of soldiers wearing night vision goggles rappelled out of the helicopters. Several cars in the street exploded as though hit by rocket launchers.

I later learned that the whole village had been rigged with pyrotechnics. Explosions were taking place all around us, including near the top of the house I was in. The air was filled with gunfire. I knew they were firing sim rounds, but it didn't sound very "sim."

Then came the flash-bangs. A 9-banger was thrown into the abandoned house I was in, which is when my amygdala took over. Without making any conscious decision to do so, I found myself running and looking for something to dive under.

I had often wondered if I was a fight guy or a flight guy. Now I knew. I didn't have the training, the tools, the technology, or the testosterone to capture the opponent. It didn't matter how much I tried to psyche myself up. There was no battle plan, and I lost before the first shot was fired.

## CAPTURE THE ENEMY

Picture a highly trained special forces operative, decked out in full gear, night vision goggles, the works. They're moving silently through enemy territory, every one of their senses on high alert. Their mission? To capture a high-value target. But here's the kicker: They're not going in guns blazing. No, this is about precision, strategy, and unwavering focus.

Special ops is a helpful way to think about 2 Corinthians 10:5: "We demolish arguments and every pretension that sets itself up against the knowledge of God, and we take captive every thought to make it obedient to Christ."

The phrase "take captive" comes from the Greek word *aichmalotizo*— a military term that means to capture an enemy combatant or to lead a prisoner away. Paul is using warfare imagery to describe our struggle against harmful thoughts. We are to treat our thoughts as if they were enemy soldiers in a spiritual battle. We are not to negotiate with them or let them roam free, but rather to decisively take them prisoner. Adopting this strategy empowers us to take an active role in our mental processes rather than being passive victims of our thoughts.

The Greek word for "thought"? It's *noema*, which refers to the mind, understanding, or thought processes. So we're not just talking about individual thoughts here; we're focused on our entire thought patterns.

Paul is essentially saying, "Hey, your mind is a battlefield, and those thoughts that go against God's truth? They're the enemy. Your job is to capture them and make them fall in line with what Christ says."

## PLAY-DOH BRAINS

How exactly do we capture these thoughts?

I mean, have you *tried* to control your thoughts? One minute you're focused on your Bible study, the next you're wondering what's for dinner, and then suddenly you're replaying that embarrassing thing you did in high school.

Throughout the book, I've been talking about this thing called neuroplasticity and how our brains can rewire themselves based on our thought patterns. It's like our brains are Play-Doh, constantly being shaped and reshaped by what we think about most.

When we consistently capture negative thoughts and replace them with positive ones, we create new neural pathways. Over time, this can break the mold of old thinking patterns and allow us to think in new and healthier ways.

So Paul's advice isn't just spiritually sound; it's backed by science. When we take our thoughts captive, we're not just obeying a biblical command; we are reshaping our brains.

Let's get practical. How do we do this? How do we become thought-capturing warriors? Remember our special ops analogy? Let's play that out:

1. **Reconnaissance:** Before operatives can capture their target, they need to know the lay of the land. They need to be aware of their surroundings. For us, this means becoming aware of our thought patterns. In the next section, we'll talk about some common thought patterns our culture tries to mold us into. For now, let's talk about what reconnaissance might look like in real life.

Sarah has struggled with anxiety for years. Her mind is constantly racing with "what ifs?" and worst-case scenarios. The first step in taking those thoughts captive is simply to notice them—not to judge them or try to change them yet, but just to become aware of them. Sarah might start keeping a thought journal. Every time she notices an anxious thought, she jots it down. "What if I fail this presentation?" "What if my kids get sick?" "What if we can't pay the bills this month?" Just the act of noticing and naming these thoughts is the first step in taking them captive.

2. **Identify the target:** Our special ops agents don't try to capture *everyone* in enemy territory. That would be overwhelming and ineffective. They have a specific target. In the same way, not all thoughts need to be taken captive in the same moment. We need to learn to recognize the thoughts that oppose God's truth.

   Back to real life . . . As Sarah reviews her thought journal, she begins to see patterns. She realizes that many of her anxious thoughts start with "What if . . ." and often involve things that are either unlikely to happen or completely out of her control. Sarah gets specific and identifies her "what if" thoughts as the target.

3. **Stealth approach:** Here's where many of us go wrong. When we notice a negative thought, our instinct is to fight it head-on. *Stop thinking that!* we tell ourselves. But have you noticed that the more you try not to think about something, the more you think about it? It's like my telling you, "Whatever you do, don't think about a giraffe riding a Harley." What are you thinking about right now?

   Instead, our special ops approach is stealthy. Sarah quietly observes the thought without overtly engaging it. Instead of attacking it head-on and calling the thought stupid, she's stealthier. She pauses to make observations. She learns to notice the anxious thought and sneak up on it by asking questions: *Where is this thought coming from? How long have I had it? How is it making me feel? Where does it tend to show up?*

4. **Precision capture:** This is where the real action happens. Our

operatives don't use brute force to capture their target; they use precision, strategy, and the right tools. In our case, it will be tools such as Scripture, prayer, and counsel from a trusted friend.

So maybe as a result of her stealth approach in asking questions about her negative thought, Sarah identifies a recurring anxious thought, maybe something like, *What if I fail this presentation and lose my job?* Now it's time for the precision capture. She surrounds this thought with truth:

» **Scripture:** She remembers Philippians 4:6–7: "Do not be anxious about anything, but in every situation, by prayer and petition, with thanksgiving, present your requests to God. And the peace of God, which transcends all understanding, will guard your hearts and your minds in Christ Jesus."

» **Prayer:** She takes a moment to pray: *God, I'm feeling anxious about this presentation. I surrender this worry to you. Please give me your peace and help me to do my best.*

» **Truth:** She reminds herself of the facts: *I've prepared well for this presentation. Even if it doesn't go perfectly, one presentation isn't going to cost me my job. And even if the worst happened and I lost my job, God has always provided for me and will continue to do so. Besides, my identity is not in this position.*

5. **Secure and redirect:** Once our operatives have captured their target, they don't just leave them there; they secure them and lead them away. In the same way, once we've captured a thought, we need to transform it by aligning it with God's truth.

In Sarah's case, she might conclude, *I trust God with the outcome of this presentation and with my career. I'll do my best to honor him with my work and leave the results in his hands.*

To help us get the hang of taking our thoughts captive, let's apply this battle plan to a few more hypothetical situations. Stick with me on this, because at the end of the chapter, you'll be invited to take thoughts captive on your own.

Meet Jack. Jack has struggled with anger issues his whole life. He has tried anger management classes and learned to count to ten, but the rage always seems to bubble just beneath the surface. Let's see how Jack might apply our special ops approach:

1. **Reconnaissance:** Jack starts paying attention to his emotions. He notices he often gets angry in traffic, when his kids are overly rambunctious, and when his wife asks him to do chores after he comes home from a long day at work.

2. **Identify the target:** Jack realizes many of his angry thoughts revolve around feeling disrespected or inconvenienced.

3. **Stealth approach:** The next time Jack is stuck in traffic and feels his anger rising, instead of engaging with it, he pauses to ask questions about it: *Where is this emotion coming from? How long have I had it? How is it making me feel? Where does it tend to show up?* And so he observes it, *Ah, there's that feeling of anger. My hands are clenching the steering wheel. My jaw is tight.* By observing what's happening, he is engaging the part of his brain called the orbital frontal cortex, which helps regulate his emotions.

4. **Precision capture:** Jack decides to focus on his anger in traffic. He uses these tools:

   » **Scripture:** He memorizes Proverbs 14:29: "Whoever is patient has great understanding, but one who is quick-tempered displays folly."

   » **Prayer:** He prays, *God, I'm feeling angry right now. Please help me to respond with patience instead of anger.*

   » **Truth:** He gets perspective by reminding himself, *This traffic isn't a personal attack on me. Everyone else is delayed too. Getting angry won't make the traffic move any faster.*

5. **Secure and redirect:** Jack transforms his angry thoughts. Instead of *These idiots are making me late!* he thinks, *This is an opportunity to practice patience. I can use this time to pray or listen to worship music.*

Over time, as Jack consistently practices this, he finds his angry outbursts becoming less frequent and less intense. He's not just managing his behavior; he's transforming his thought patterns.

One more example. Lisa has struggled with feelings of worthlessness for as long as she can remember. She has tried positive affirmations, but they've always felt hollow. Here's how Lisa applies our special ops approach:

1. **Reconnaissance:** Lisa starts by observing her own emotions. She realizes that she feels stressed out when she is on social media, struggling at work, or alone on a Friday night.

2. **Identify the target:** Lisa identifies that her emotions are triggered by thoughts of worthlessness, thoughts that would not be in line with God's view of her.

3. **Stealth approach:** The next time Lisa finds herself scrolling through Instagram and feeling worthless, she doesn't try to fight the feeling; she takes a step back and asks questions of herself: *Where is this feeling coming from? How long have I had it? How is it making me feel? Where does it tend to show up?* She becomes aware of a feeling of worthlessness and the tightness in her chest. She realizes that she is comparing herself with others and basing her value on her accomplishments, appearance, and relationships. She acknowledges that she grew up needing to perform to receive acceptance from her parents.

4. **Precision capture:** Lisa decides to focus on the thoughts that come up when she's on social media. She uses these tools:
   » **Scripture:** She memorizes Psalm 139:14: "I praise you because I am fearfully and wonderfully made; your works are wonderful, I know that full well."
   » **Prayer:** She prays, *God, I'm feeling worthless right now. Please help me to see myself as you see me.*
   » **Truth:** She reminds herself, *Social media shows highlight reels, not real life. My worth isn't determined by how I measure up to others' carefully curated posts.*

5. **Secure and redirect:** Lisa transforms her thoughts of worthlessness. Instead of *Everyone else has it all together. I'm such a mess*, she thinks, *I am fearfully and wonderfully made by God. My worth comes from him, not from what others think of me or how I compare to others.*

I want to be clear. Taking our thoughts captive isn't a quick fix or a onetime thing; it's an ongoing process, a lifetime battle. But what's amazing is that the more we do it, the easier it becomes. Remember neuroplasticity? You are reshaping your brain. The more you practice capturing your thoughts, the more your brain will create pathways that will make it easier to capture thoughts in the future.

## SQUAD PATROL: THE SPIRIT AND THE SAINTS

In this battle of the mind don't ever think, *I'm all alone.* You are not out there by yourself practicing the power of positive thinking. This isn't you sitting by yourself in an ice bath practicing mind control.

Imagine being a special forces operative tasked with a critical mission deep in enemy territory. In your imagination are you alone?

In the battle for your mind, you should never be alone. Look at 2 Corinthians 10:5 again: "We demolish arguments and every pretension that sets itself up against the knowledge of God, and we take captive every thought to make it obedient to Christ."

Notice that Paul uses the word *we* rather than *I* or *you*. This is a team operation. You are taking your thoughts captive, but you're doing it with the help of the Holy Spirit. Jesus called the Holy Spirit our helper. One of the ways the Spirit helps us is by guiding our thoughts. Jesus said to his disciples that the Holy Spirit "will teach you all things and will remind you of everything I have said to you" (John 14:26).

The Holy Spirit will bring supernatural awareness to our thoughts, help us remember Bible verses, and teach us how to apply them to our lives. He's in this struggle with us. On this journey, there will be times when we'll have negative, lustful, or vengeful thoughts, and out of nowhere a Bible verse will pop into our heads. You may think to yourself, *Where did that come from?* It came from the Holy Spirit, and when that happens, and it will happen, let it be a powerful reminder that you are not alone. He's got your back and will never leave your side.

The Holy Spirit helps us by teaching, reminding, and strengthening us. Romans 8:26 reads, "The Spirit helps us in our weakness." When you're feeling overwhelmed by your thoughts, when you feel like your thoughts have pinned you back and are holding you down, remember that the Holy Spirit is there to give you strength. Call on him for help.

You're not alone because you have the Spirit *and* you have the saints. We'll call this squad support. Proverbs 27:17 reads, "As iron sharpens iron, so one person sharpens another."

First Thessalonians 5:11 instructs us, "Encourage one another and build each other up, just as in fact you are doing."

I have a pastor friend who I check in with a few times a month. We ask each other a few challenging personal questions. If one of us is struggling with angry, lustful, or prideful thoughts, we'll admit to the trial and ask for prayer. It's not unusual for one of us to send a message like this:

> Hey, I got a super-critical and harsh email from someone in the church. I can't get it out of my head and I feel angry, but I know I'm just hurt. I want to send a harsh email back, but I know that wouldn't help. Say a prayer for me, and I'm going to send you my response to look at before I send it to them.

Or

> Hey, I'm at a hotel by myself tonight. I'm going to be tempted to waste time scrolling on my phone, and I may be tempted to look at some pictures that would take my thoughts in the wrong direction. Say a prayer for me tonight and ask me tomorrow how it went.

Or

Hey, I came home today and snapped at my wife. I was not tender or gentle with her. Pray for me to take my thoughts captive and to be quick to listen, slow to speak, and slow to become angry.

Something happens when we do this for each other. I'm convinced that his prayers for me at the right time have the power to break strongholds I can't break alone.

How does this work in real life? Let's revisit our examples:

1. **Sarah and her anxiety:** Sarah doesn't just try to capture anxious thoughts on her own; she asks the Holy Spirit for help in recognizing anxiety-driven thoughts. She memorizes Philippians 4:6–7 and asks the Spirit to bring it to her mind when she's anxious. She also shares her struggle with her small group. They pray for her regularly and check in on her progress. One friend texts her encouraging Bible verses each morning.

2. **Jack and his anger:** Jack invites the Holy Spirit into his anger management process. He asks for the Spirit's help in staying calm and responding with love. He also asks his men's group for support. They hold him accountable, asking him weekly about his anger triggers and responses. He identifies one friend he can call or text whenever he feels his temper rising.

3. **Lisa and her self-worth issues:** Lisa begins each day by asking the Holy Spirit to help her see herself as God sees her. She asks for help in recognizing thoughts that contradict her true identity in Christ. She also opens up to a trusted mentor at church who prays with her, encourages her with truth from Scripture, and gently challenges Lisa's negative self-talk when she hears it.

You can do this too. Please don't treat taking your thoughts captive as a solo mission.

# YOUR MISSION, SHOULD YOU CHOOSE TO ACCEPT IT

This thought-capturing process is mind renewal in action. It doesn't just change our behaviors; it changes the very way we think. And that changes the way we live.

I know what you might be thinking: *This sounds great in theory, but my thoughts are really messed up. You don't know what's going on inside my head.* If that's what you're thinking, take that thought captive and run it through our special ops process.

Imagine what your life might look like if you captured those anxious thoughts and replaced them with God's peace. Envision how your relationships might improve if you were to capture angry thoughts and replace them with expressions of patience and understanding. Imagine how differently you might see yourself if you captured thoughts of worthlessness and replaced them with the truth of your inestimable value in God's eyes.

This is the power of taking our thoughts captive. It's not just about controlling our thoughts; it's about allowing God to transform our minds. It's about bringing every thought under the lordship of Christ.

So here's my challenge: Go on your own reconnaissance mission. Pay attention to your thoughts. Jot them down if that helps. Start to identify which thoughts need to be taken captive. And then start practicing the capture process. Use Scripture, prayer, and truth to capture those thoughts and align them with God's truth.

## COMBAT READY

Below is a tool designed to help apply the principles of taking thoughts captive in our daily lives. We looked at some examples, using thoughts of anxiety, anger, and worthlessness. Now it's time to do the application on your own. I encourage you to work through these questions thoughtfully.

1. **Reconnaissance:** (1) Pay attention to a particular thought pattern. What negative or unhelpful thoughts do you notice recurring?

(2) In what situations do these thoughts typically arise? (3) How do these thoughts make you feel emotionally and physically?

2. **Identify the target:** (1) Out of all the thoughts you observed, which ones do you see as the most damaging or contrary to God's truth? (2) Why do you think these particular thoughts have such a strong hold on you? (3) Can you identify any common themes or triggers for these thoughts?

3. **Stealth approach:** The next time you notice one of these target thoughts or difficult feelings, try to observe them without engaging. Ask yourself, (1) *Where is this emotion coming from?* (2) *How long have I had it?* (3) *How is it making me feel?* (4) *Where does it tend to show up?* Ponder what may have changed in you emotionally or physically when you took time to think about your thoughts.

4. **Precision capture:** Choose one of your identified target thoughts and respond to the following: (1) What Scripture verse or passage speaks truth against this thought? (2) Write a brief prayer asking God for help in dealing with this specific thought. (3) What factual truths can you use to counter this thought?

5. **Secure and redirect:** (1) How can you rephrase your target thought to align with God's truth? (2) Have you written the thought down so you can intentionally think a new thought? (3) How might consistently redirecting this thought change your life?

Give it a try right now. On the blank lines at the end of the chapter, identify a repeating harmful thought and then apply the above five steps. To further help you apply these strategies:

**Training exercises:** (1) Set a reminder on your phone to do a quick "thought check" three times a day. (2) Keep a thought journal for a week. What patterns do you observe? (3) Memorize one Scripture verse a week that addresses a recurring negative thought. How does having this verse at your disposal change your response to the thought?

**Debriefing:** (1) After trying this process for a week, what changes are you noticing in your thinking, behavior, and emotions? (2) What part of the process did you find most challenging? Why? (3) How can you continue to practice taking thoughts captive in your daily life?

**Squad support:** (1) Who can you ask to support you and hold you accountable in this process? (2) How can your church community or small group help you in this quest to renew your mind?

Remember, taking thoughts captive is an ongoing mission. Be patient with yourself, celebrate small victories, and keep practicing. You may lose a few battles, but don't give up. With God's help, you will win the war.

## CHAPTER 10

# THINK ABOUT THESE THINGS

## DEVELOPING A DIVINE FOCUS

Isn't it crazy how two people can look at the same thing but see very different things. It's confusing and more than a little annoying. "If you're looking at what I'm looking at, why don't you see what I'm seeing?"

A weird but poignant example was "Dressageddon" in 2015, when the world stopped to debate the color of a striped dress on the internet. Was it black and blue? Or gold and white? Very quickly, the picture of the dress was getting 840,000 views *per minute*, and before long, more than ten million people had tweeted about the dress. #Dressgate was dividing friends and families. Teams started forming. "I'm team black and blue." "Count me in on team gold and white."

From my perspective the dress was black and blue, and in real life, it turned out I was right. Some of you who were #TeamGoldAndWhite refuse to believe that. That's understandable. More people thought it was white and gold. Most people were wrong.

Since the dress scandal that rocked the world, several scientists have explained why people saw different colors, and the answer is basically all about *perspective*. Your perspective shapes the way you see what you see.

Turns out when we looked at the dress, we were subconsciously making assumptions about light, and those assumptions, which we don't even realize we're making, are determining what we believe we see.

This dynamic is real *all* the time in *all* kinds of ways.

When we think about something, we're making all kinds of subconscious assumptions that shape our perspectives, and those subconscious thoughts determine what we believe we're seeing. That's why two people can look at the same thing, and based on their perspective, they see the same thing but reach very different conclusions.

It's ~~annoying~~ interesting when what we differ on is the color of an online dress, but what about other thoughts we have where the stakes are much higher? For example, when you experience massive disappointment, what do you see?

Process for a moment how you think about events that have happened or perhaps will happen in your life:

**A difficult breakup:** Do you see the event as the end of your love life or as a chance to meet someone who is a better fit?

**A challenge at work:** Do you see it as a stressful burden or as an opportunity for growth?

**A forced relocation:** Do you see it as a disruptive upheaval or as an exciting adventure?

**A surprise pregnancy:** Do you see it as an unexpected disruption or as an astonishing blessing?

**A financial setback:** Do you see it as a devastating blow or as an invigorating challenge?

**A critical review:** Do you see it as a personal attack or as a way to improve yourself.

**A health challenge:** Do you see it as a hopeless battle or as a wake-up call to help you live more fully.

What you see in these moments is largely determined by your subconscious perspective, which is largely shaped by your repeated thoughts. Think of it as a self-reinforcing cycle.

Here's how it works:

- **Thoughts:** We have thoughts about something.
- **Perspective:** Our thoughts shape our perspectives.
- **Interpretation:** We interpret events through the lens of our perspectives.
- **Experience:** These interpretations shape our experiences.
- **Memory:** We form memories based on these experiences.
- **Reinforcement:** These memories reinforce our original thoughts.
- **Repeat:** The cycle continues, strengthening with each iteration.

Let's play this out. Hailey had always considered herself unlucky. This belief stemmed from a series of disappointing experiences in her childhood, including losing a school election by a handful of votes closely followed by failing to make the soccer team when everyone told her she should have. These events shaped her perspective, convincing her that the world was inherently unfair to her.

One Monday morning, Hailey woke up late for work. As she rushed to get ready, she thought to herself, *Of course this would happen to me. I'm always unlucky.* This thought reinforced her negative perspective.

On her way to work, Hailey encountered heavy traffic. Through the lens of her "unlucky" perspective, she interpreted the slowdown as another sign of her perpetual misfortune rather than as a common occurrence in city life. This interpretation shaped her experience of the morning commute, turning it into a stressful and frustrating ordeal.

By the time she arrived at work, she was in a bad mood. Her boss asked her to take on a new project. Instead of seeing this as an opportunity, Hailey's negative perspective led her to interpret it as an unfair burden. *Why me?* she thought. *It's just my luck to get extra work dumped on me.*

That evening, as she reflected on her day, Hailey formed memories that aligned with her perspective of misfortune. She focused on the late start, the traffic, and the extra work, ignoring any positive aspects of her day, such as the tastiness of the muffin that a coworker had saved for her, the compliment she received on her presentation, or her boss entrusting and empowering her to take on a new assignment.

These memories served to reinforce Hailey's original thoughts about her unluckiness. She went to bed thinking, *Just another typical unlucky day in my life.*

The next morning, Hailey woke up with the same thought: *I'm so unlucky.* And so the cycle began again, her thoughts shaping her perspective, her perspective coloring her interpretations, her interpretations influencing her experiences, which in turn created memories that reinforced her initial thoughts.

Weeks passed, and Hailey's belief in her own bad luck only grew stronger. Each perceived instance of calamity added another layer to her negative perspective, making it increasingly difficult to recognize positive events or alternative interpretations.

## THE PERSPECTIVE PARADIGM

Perspective shapes our reality. We see this in the life of Jesus. Take, for example, his perspective on Matthew, the tax collector. In first-century Jewish society, tax collectors were viewed as traitors and sinners, collaborators with the Roman occupiers who often extorted extra money for themselves. But Jesus looked beyond his profession and public persona and saw a potential disciple.

Jesus viewed things and people differently, and so can we.

While our perspectives can be shaped by our subconscious or

unintentional thoughts, it doesn't have to be that way. As we take our thoughts captive and choose to intentionally think about the right things, we can determine our perspective and choose how we view things.

That's not just wishful thinking; it's scientifically proven. Psychologists call it cognitive reappraisal. It's our ability to reframe the meaning of what we are experiencing.

Scientists have conducted all kinds of neuroimaging studies in which they have shown that there are consistent patterns of neural activation. When someone chooses to change their perspective, the studies show an increased activity in prefrontal regions involved in cognitive control and decreased activity in the emotion-driven regions of the brain. This means that our brains will go to work for us when we decide we want to look at something in a different way.

We can "game" our perspectives and choose one that is good and godly and moves us toward the person we want to become.

Here's a simple example. In a study at the State University of New York at Buffalo, subjects were asked to complete the following sentence five times: "I'm glad I'm not a _____." What happened? They experienced a measurable increase in their level of satisfaction with their lives. A second group of subjects was asked to complete this sentence five times: "I wish I were a _____." The result? A measurable *decrease* in the level of satisfaction they had with their lives.[1] Did any of these volunteer's lives actually change? No, but the way they looked at their lives did.

How do you look at your life? At your problems? At what's going on in the world? At the issues in your church? At your job?

We believe in a God who is all-knowing, all-powerful, and all-awesome. Our God brings victory out of failure, good out of bad, and life out of death. Ultimately, he is in control of everything. If all that is true, and it is, we can choose a faith-filled, life-giving, love-inducing, peace-that-transcends-all-understanding perspective.

But—here let's remember the law of cognition—whether or not we have the perspective we want to have is not determined so much by a choice we make as it is by the thoughts we think.

# TEN VERSUS TWO

Israel had spent four hundred-plus years as slaves in Egypt, and then they called out to God, asking him to deliver them. God tells them he will free them from slavery and lead them to the land that was promised to them.

Through Moses, God sends plagues on Egypt, but spares the Israelites living in Egypt from being ravaged by them. Finally, Pharaoh is compelled to let the Israelites go.

The Israelites begin their journey out of Egypt toward the promised land, but Pharaoh has a change of heart and sends his armies to pursue them. They are hot on the Israelites' heels, and the Red Sea is looming right in front of the people of Israel. They are trapped. But the people watch as God splits the Red Sea, creating a highway for them to walk through. When the Egyptian army comes after them, the sea collapses on them. As the Israelites continue their journey through the wilderness, God provides for them in undeniably miraculous ways.

The Israelites have had front-row seats to see the incredible power and provision of God. Finally they are standing at the precipice of the promised land, the land God promised to them hundreds of years earlier through Abraham. Generation after generation had anticipated this moment, and it has now arrived. They are looking at it right in front of them.

The biblical account reads, "The LORD said to Moses, 'Send some men to explore the land of Canaan, which I am giving to the Israelites. From each ancestral tribe send one of its leaders'" (Numbers 13:1–2).

Remember, this is the promised land. God tells Moses to send some men into the *promised* land—Not the "*I'm contemplating it* land" or the "*We'll see* land" or the "*I'll consider it* land" or the "*We'll talk about it later* land."

It's the promised land. God tells Moses that it's the land "which I am giving to the Israelites." Like, it's already been decided. Send some men to explore the land I've already determined to give to you.

God did not tell them, "I want you to go into the land and see what you think, decide if you feel like I'm capable of giving it to you. I want you to come back and do a SWOT analysis and a risk assessment. Oh, and you should also make a pie chart indicating the likelihood of success. I'll take all of your information to Jesus and the Holy Spirit. We'll talk it over, and then we'll let you know what we decide."

No.

The spies are sent to investigate, but the land had already been promised. The twelve spies are chosen, and Moses gives them their assignment, ending with these words: "Do your best to bring back some of the fruit of the land" (Numbers 13:20). Moses tells the spies what to look for when they go in the land—fruit. Fruit is what is good. Fruit is evidence of what God has said.

The twelve spies walk off, and everyone is waving—and then everyone waits . . . for forty days. I don't know, but I would have assumed this reconnaissance mission would take maybe four days. They are gone for forty.

My hunch is that during these forty days, the people's anxiety levels may have risen. They begin to wonder, *Are they ever coming back, and what will they tell us if they do?*

The twelve men finally return with their report, and their report provides a great example of *perspective*. Remember, it's not what we see; it's what we *think* we see. Our perspective is all-important; it shapes our reality.

> We entered the land you sent us to explore, and it is indeed a bountiful country—a land flowing with milk and honey. Here is the kind of fruit it produces. But the people living there are powerful, and their towns are large and fortified. We even saw giants there, the descendants of Anak!
>
> NUMBERS 13:27–28 NLT

Their report essentially goes like this: "Just like God said, the land is awesome. And just like you asked, we brought fruit back. But . . ."

But is always a dangerous word when it comes to our perspective. Too often, it's, "I know what God said, and I know what he promised, but . . ." and that's exactly what happens here.

"But the people are too powerful. The cities are too fortified. We saw descendants of Anak—they're giants. They're way too big."

Ten spies give a negative report. Two spies, Caleb and Joshua, have a different perspective. They all saw the same things, but they saw it differently.

> But Caleb tried to quiet the people as they stood before Moses. "Let's go at once to take the land," he said. "We can certainly conquer it!"
>
> **NUMBERS 13:30 NLT**

They see the same things, but their reality is determined by their perspective. Ten come back reporting, "We can't. It's too much." Two return saying, "It's ours. Let's go!"

The ten aren't sure their negative view is going to win the day, so they give what might be the first recorded telling of #fakenews:

> But the other men who had explored the land with him disagreed. "We can't go up against them! They are stronger than we are!" So they spread this bad report about the land among the Israelites: "The land we traveled through and explored will devour anyone who goes to live there. All the people we saw were huge. We even saw giants there, the descendants of Anak. Next to them we felt like grasshoppers, and that's what they thought, too!"
>
> **NUMBERS 13:31–33 NLT**

Here we have another problem of perspective. If a grasshopper stands about one inch tall and the average Israelite man was foot five eight, that's a ratio of 68 to 1. That means the men living in the promised land would have been about four thousand feet tall.

When we fail to take our thoughts captive, they shape our perspectives in ways that exaggerate the struggles we are facing and underestimate the power of God.

How do the people of Israel respond to the negativity of the ten spies?

Do they fight back? "No, we are children of the living God. He has gotten us through everything we need to go through. Miracles are our history, and more miracles are coming!"

Nope.

> Then the whole community began weeping aloud, and they cried all night. Their voices rose in a great chorus of protest against Moses and Aaron. "If only we had died in Egypt, or even here in the wilderness!" they complained. "Why is the LORD taking us to this country only to have us die in battle? Our wives and our little ones will be carried off as plunder! Wouldn't it be better for us to return to Egypt?" Then they plotted among themselves, "Let's choose a new leader and go back to Egypt!"
>
> NUMBERS 14:1–4 NLT

Negativity is like an infection that spreads. Pessimism becomes its own pandemic. Everyone is complaining and critical and ready to book their return trip to slavery in Egypt. But the other two spies, Joshua and Caleb, try to shift their perspective:

> Two of the men who had explored the land, Joshua son of Nun and Caleb son of Jephunneh, tore their clothing. They said to all the people of Israel, "The land we traveled through and explored is a wonderful land! And if the LORD is pleased with us, he will bring us safely into that land and give it to us. It is a rich land flowing with milk and honey. Do not rebel against the LORD, and don't be afraid of the people of the land. They are only helpless prey to us! They have no protection, but the LORD is with us! Don't be afraid of them!"
>
> NUMBERS 14:6–9

Do you see how they looked at the same things but saw it completely differently? Ten come back: "We're like grasshoppers who will get stepped on!" Two return: "They are helpless prey to us. We'll step on them."

Why do the two spies have so much confidence? Because "the LORD is with us!"

Our perspective shapes our lives, and our perspective is shaped by what we think about. What do you think Joshua and Caleb had been thinking about? It seems obvious—the miraculous way God had led them out of slavery . . . and the plagues he had sent upon the Egyptians . . . and the way he parted the Red Sea . . . and the manna he provided for them in the wilderness . . . and the water he made to gush out of the rock when they were thirsty. If God could do all that, how could he not do all this?

What do you think the other ten spies had been thinking about? Obviously not all that.

The ten see only problems; the two see only the presence and power of a God who had made promises he will always keep.

## THREE QUESTIONS

I invite you to reflect on a few questions that can help you determine how what you think about shapes your perspective. These questions reveal where your current perspective is coming from and how you can change it going forward.

### 1. What Am I Looking For?

Dr. John Gottman is one of the world's foremost marriage researchers and clinical psychologists. He studies why some marriages succeed while others don't—why some are "marriage masters" and others "marriage disasters."

After years of studying more than forty thousand couples, Gottman can now predict with incredible accuracy whether a couple will get divorced. How? He pinpoints a few key factors that separate marriage masters from disasters.[2] As you might guess, one factor is perspective.

Dr. Gottman says marriage masters are always scanning their social environment for things to appreciate and to say thank you for. Disasters are the opposite. They are looking for their partners' mistakes, for ways they need to change and areas they can improve.

Gottman explains that masters have a "positive sentiment override."[3] They choose the best possible explanation for what their spouse says, does, or the mood they're in. Disasters have a "negative sentiment override." They see the same things as the people with happy, successful marriages, but they assume the worst.

You're talking but your spouse isn't listening? A master with positive sentiment override might think, *My spouse is a little distracted. They may be dealing with something heavy or feeling stressed.* A disaster with negative sentiment override assumes, *My spouse doesn't care about me. He's such a jerk,* or *She's always like that.*

It's often not what happens in the marriage that determines the health of the marriage; it's how the partners in the marriage *perceive* what happens. Their perception is dictated by what they're looking for and choosing to think about.

What should we be looking for in life? What should we be thinking about so that we can have the best possible perspective? "Finally, brothers and sisters, whatever is true, whatever is noble, whatever is right, whatever is pure, whatever is lovely, whatever is admirable—if anything is excellent or praiseworthy—think about such things" (Philippians 4:8).

*That's* what we're looking for. Paul gives a filter for our thoughts that will shape our perspectives and determine our lives. A few years ago, I spent a month traveling in a country that had limited access to clean water. My wife bought me a water bottle that cost 150 dollars because it can filter any kind of water. I can take water from a mud puddle, run it through the filter, and drink it out of the bottle moments later. This filter can strain out and eliminate viruses, bacteria, and parasites and give me clean water to drink.

Think of this list in Philippians 4 as a filter to run your thoughts through when you take them captive:

Is this thought *true*?
Is this thought *noble*?
Is this thought *right*?

Is this thought *pure*?

Is this thought *lovely*?

Is this thought *admirable*?

Is this thought *excellent*?

Is this thought *praiseworthy*?

Because we have an amazing God who has done so much for us, we can live with a positive sentiment override that allows us to see and think about what's true, lovely, and praiseworthy.

## A PARABLE: THE SMUDGED WINDOW

Kristen had always dreamed of visiting the picturesque coastal town of Seaview. She had seen countless online photos of its stunning cliffs, pristine beaches, and vibrant sunsets. Finally, after years of saving, she booked a weeklong stay at a highly rated Airbnb perched on the cliffs overlooking the ocean.

As soon as she arrived, Kristen rushed to the large picture window that dominated the living room wall. This was the view everyone raved about in the reviews. But as she approached, her excitement quickly turned to disappointment. There, right in the center of the window, was a small but noticeable smudge.

Kristen tried to look past it, but her eyes kept being drawn back to that imperfection. She spent the next hour trying to clean it off, but it seemed to be between the windowpanes, impossible to reach.

For the rest of her stay, Kristen found herself fixated on that smudge. When she looked out the window, instead of seeing the vast expanse of the sparkling ocean, the rugged beauty of the cliffs, or the glorious colors of the sunset, all she could focus on was that small, blurry spot. Her photos showcased the smudge rather than the view. The more she saw it, the more she saw it. She finally shut the curtains so she wouldn't have to see the smudge anymore.

She spent most of her vacation indoors, feeling cheated and frustrated. She barely noticed the sound of the waves or the fresh sea breeze when she briefly ventured out.

On the last day of her stay, Kristen left a scathing review: "I don't understand why everyone raves about the view from this place. All I could see was a dirty window. The beauty of Seaview is greatly exaggerated."

As Kristen got in her car to leave, a young couple was just arriving to check into the Airbnb. The woman gasped with excitement as she got out of the car, pointing at the view in awe. "Look at that sunset. It's even more beautiful than in the pictures!"

Kristen glanced in her rearview mirror as she was driving away, hoping to catch a glimpse of a spectacular golden sun sinking into a violet and pink sky, but she couldn't help but notice that on her rearview mirror there was a smudge.

What are you looking for? Not what are you looking *at*, but what are you looking *for*? What you look for is what you'll find.

The twelve spies were told to look for fruit. Fruit is evidence that God can be trusted.

Do you look for what's good? Do you look for fruit, or do you look for frustrations? Whichever one you look for, you'll find it.

Do you look for opportunities or obstacles? For beauty or barriers? For what's possible or for problems?

The twelve spies looked at the same thing, but ten looked through the lens of fear and saw problems. Two looked through the lens of faith and saw promise.

I've noticed that the lens of fear is a close-up lens. It causes tunnel vision, focusing only on what's right in front of us and making obstacles seem bigger than they are. The lens of faith is a wide-angle lens. It provides the big picture, refusing to leave God out and keeping everything in proper perspective.

How do we shift from the close-up lens of fear to the wide-angle lens of faith? We choose to intentionally look for fruit.

My wife has been a great example of this. During the COVID-19 shutdown, when it seemed like everyone's perspective was turning negative, DesiRae began each day by writing in a gratitude journal. She examined her life and wrote down three things for which she was grateful. She started every morning by looking for the fruit.

DesiRae starts the day by taking her thoughts captive and intentionally looking for and thinking about what is excellent and praiseworthy. What do *you* look for? Whatever it is, that's what you'll find.

I'll be honest, it's not always easy. A few years back, my struggle came into full display as I was writing a sermon on this very topic. As I prepared to teach on looking for and fixing our thoughts on what is true, noble, pure, and lovely, my home was robbed . . . for the second time in five months. The first time was while we were at church on a Sunday morning. I was frustrated because I thought, *They knew we were in church!* That was discouraging but we kept a good attitude about it. We just filed a police report and said to ourselves, *These things happen.*

Then it happened *again*. This time, my attitude wasn't so great. The thieves took my computer and iPad. The work I had recently done hadn't been backed up. I was frustrated and angry and feeling sorry for myself. I didn't mean to complain, but I was complaining.

One day that week, I was still stuck in my sour attitude, still complaining to anyone who would listen, when my assistant came in and said, "Hey, I want to let you know about a situation that needs some prayer." She went on to tell me about a young missionary couple our church supports who had a newborn baby in Somalia. They had been arrested and put in prison for sharing their faith. I stopped what I was doing and prayed for this young couple. And . . . my lens shifted a little. It gave me a better perspective on my own frustrations.

A little later that same day, I walked into my office, and on my desk was a book someone had sent me: *Forty Days on the Front Lines with Persecuted Christians.* I started going through it and thought, *Okay, I get it, Lord!*

I stepped out of my office and told my assistant, "My attitude hasn't been very good today. I just want to tell you I'm sorry. You know, hearing about the missionary couple in Somalia and seeing that book on my desk helped shift my perspective." I turned to walk back into my office, and she said, "I thought it might."

That's what I needed. I was focused on my smudges, and the reality was taking place in the big picture of things—what's happening around the world, what other people are living with. My perspective was off. I needed to change what I was looking for so my perspective could change, and I could see things differently.

What are you looking for?

## 2. Who Do I Listen To?

Who we listen to has a way of shaping our perspectives and determining what we see.

In the story, twelve spies come back. Ten give a fear-based, negative report; two offer a faith-based report that's highly optimistic.

Who do you listen to?

There's a lot at stake. A couple million Israelites have to decide, "Do I listen to the two or to the ten?"

I was thinking about that 10:2 negative to positive ratio, and it seems about right to me. I haven't commissioned any studies, but it feels like in our world, the 10:2 of negative to positive ratio holds true.

That is . . . a problem. It means we need to be very intentional about who or what we listen to.

If we're constantly surfing the net, watching the twenty-four-hour news cycle, flipping through TV channels, or looking through our social media feeds, we are not being inundated with that which is true, pure, noble, and praiseworthy. If we hang out with friends who are negative, critical, or love to gossip, we are not being led to think about that which is lovely, admirable, and excellent.

A whole bunch of Israelites decide to listen to the ten.

Why did they choose to listen to the faithless over the faithful, to those who ignored God rather than those who focused on him? Part of it has to be the numbers—ten to two. If ten had come back with a positive report and only two with a negative, it may well have been a different story.

The danger is if we have ten faithless, fearful, negative, critical inputs for every two faithful, fearless, positive, constructive inputs, we're likely to find our thoughts influenced in the same way the Israelites did.

Because the Israelites listen to the ten instead of the two, they have to wander in the wilderness for forty years. God tells them it will be "one year for each of the forty days you explored the land" (Numbers 14:34). Everyone in that unbelieving generation dies off, and the only two who enter the promised land forty years later are Caleb and Joshua.

Who do you listen to?

A buddy of mine got out of rehab not long ago. He said the hardest time was the overnight. He'd lie in bed, and the voices would start up. *It's too much of a mess. Things are too broken. Your wife isn't ever going to see you the same way. You can't come back from this. God has turned his back on you.*

Hearing those voices was overwhelming him, so he decided to drown them out by putting in his earbuds and listening to the song "Way Maker" on repeat. He'd sing along, praising God as a "way maker, miracle worker, promise keeper, Light in the darkness."[4] He kept listening to it, listening to it, listening to it, and over time, he developed a positive sentiment override. What he listened to changed his thoughts, and his thoughts changed his perspective.

### 3. What Will I Dwell On?

In 2002, *A Beautiful Mind* won the Academy Award for Best Picture. The movie was about Nobel Prize–winner John Nash, a genius mathematician who studied at Princeton, taught at MIT, and was recruited to decipher Soviet codes for the United States government during the height of the Cold War.

Nash, who was tortured by paranoid schizophrenia, constantly heard accusing voices and couldn't discern reality from hallucination. He became unable to do math, care for his young son, or be intimate with his wife.

Nash was determined to overcome his mental illness and eventually did. In 1994, Thomas King from the Nobel Committee met with Nash to assess his mental state. Nash told King, "I am crazy. I take the newer medications, but I still see things that are not here. I just choose not to acknowledge them. Like a diet of the mind, I just choose not to indulge certain appetites."[5]

I like that. Like a diet of the mind. I choose not to indulge certain appetites.

Most of us have had times when we were unhappy with our physical fitness. In those moments, we realize we have a choice about what we eat. We may not have been using this freedom to choose, but we do have it. And so we may choose to go on a diet. From now on, I will not eat . . . carbs . . . sweets . . . frozen burritos. It may be difficult, but it makes perfect sense to us—we choose what we eat.

We also have the freedom to choose what we think about. Yes, unwanted, intrusive thoughts will come knocking on the door of our minds, but *we choose* whether to invite them in.

Jesus told us, "Do not worry" (Matthew 6:25). He wasn't suggesting stressful things wouldn't happen in life or that anxious thoughts wouldn't come knocking, but instead was telling us to choose not to think about them. We choose to think about God, knowing, "You will keep in perfect peace all who trust in you, all whose thoughts are fixed on you!" (Isaiah 26:3 NLT).

These ideas in the Bible from ancient times are confirmed by science today. A study investigated the impact of rumination—repetitive negative thinking—on anxiety, and as you might expect, it was found that keeping our minds stuck in negative thinking exacerbates anxiety and produces high levels of worry.[6] The solution? Reduce rumination to manage your anxiety.

We choose what we think about, and we have a God who wants to empower us to make and live out the right choices. Dwell on what is true, noble, right, pure, lovely, admirable, excellent, and praiseworthy, and watch it change your perspective and your life.

My son has wanted me to change what I eat for a while, but I've told him if I do what he's asking, I won't get enough calories. He says in a whiny voice (don't tell him I said his voice was whiny), "Dad, you eat too much, and you use the excuse you need to eat more because if you don't, you're not getting enough calories. The truth is, you have plenty of calories you're just not paying attention to what you're eating." So to help me be more aware of what I eat, he has me writing in a food journal everything I put in my mouth.

It's a *lot* of *fun*. (Read that sentence in your most sarcastic voice.)

He checks my journal and asks, "What about the Reese's Pieces? And the Sour Patch Kids?"

I explain, always very patiently, that I'm not *lying* about the candy; I'm just *misremembering* about the candy.

The truth is that using a food journal has been highly illuminating. For the first time, I'm aware of what I eat, and the way my diet impacts my life finally makes sense. I'm seeing things I did not see before, because I've become aware of things I've been in the habit of overlooking.

This eye-opening (and hunger-inducing) experience got me thinking, *What if we were to apply the same principle to our thoughts? What if we could go on a "thought diet" to nourish our minds with healthier, more positive thinking?*

Just as we may not realize how many unhealthy foods we're consuming until we keep track, we often don't recognize the negative thought patterns that dominate our mental landscape. Yet by becoming aware of these patterns, we can begin to make positive changes. So I challenge you to try this thought diet. Even if you think your mental diet is already healthy, you may be surprised by what you discover. Are you ready to nourish your mind?

## The Thought Diet

1. **Thought journal:** For one week, jot down your thoughts throughout the day. Don't judge or try to change these thoughts; just record them. Think of it as your mental food diary. (See the appendix for more details about a thought journal.)

2. **Thought classification:** After a week, review your journal. Classify your thoughts into categories:
   » **"Junk food" thoughts:** negative self-talk, worries, complaints, lust, selfishness
   » **"Empty calorie" thoughts:** unproductive ruminations, excessive social media scrolling
   » **"Healthy snack" thoughts:** positive self-talk, gratitude, problem-solving
   » **"Nutrient-dense" thoughts:** Scripture meditation, worship singing, meaningful reflections

3. **Thought triggers:** Just as certain situations can trigger unhealthy eating, identify what triggers your "junk food" thoughts. Is it stress? Certain people? Particular times of the day?

4. **Thought menu:** Develop a list of go-to positive thoughts or Scriptures. These are your "healthy snacks" for getting a mental boost.

5. **Thought substitution:** When you catch yourself indulging in a "junk food" thought, consciously replace it with a healthier alternative from your "thought menu."

6. **Mindful thought eating:** Practice mindfulness. Before engaging with a thought, pause and ask, *Is this nourishing my mind?*

7. **Thought meal prep:** Start each day by consciously choosing several positive thoughts to focus on, just as you might do meal prep for healthy eating.

Take a few minutes to look back through these ideas and identify two or three that you can implement.

## CHAPTER 11

# SAY IT OUT LOUD

## THE POWER THAT SPEAKING HAS ON YOUR THINKING

D eath was everywhere. A valley of it.

Dry. Brittle. Dead bones as far as Ezekiel could see.

It was a difficult time in Israel's history. The Babylonians had invaded and captured the Israelites. Ezekiel was one of many taken into captivity and exiled to Babylon. God wanted Ezekiel to understand that power is available when God speaks his word into impossible situations.

Ezekiel shares a prophetic vision God gave him:

> The LORD took hold of me, and I was carried away by the Spirit of the
> LORD to a valley filled with bones. He led me all around among the
> bones that covered the valley floor. They were scattered everywhere
> across the ground and were completely dried out. Then he asked me,
> "Son of man, can these bones become living people again?"
>
> "O Sovereign LORD," I replied, "you alone know the answer to that."

Then he said to me, "Speak a prophetic message to these bones and say, 'Dry bones, listen to the word of the LORD! This is what the Sovereign LORD says: Look! I am going to put breath into you and make you live again! I will put flesh and muscles on you and cover you with skin. I will put breath into you, and you will come to life. Then you will know that I am the LORD.'"

EZEKIEL 37:1–6 NLT

In essence, God asks Ezekiel, "Can these dead bones live again?"

It's a great question, not just for Ezekiel, but for us as well. Something may seem beyond hope. Too dry. Too broken. Too bitter. Too ingrained. Too much. Too long. Too dead.

Your marriage may feel lifeless. Your relationship with one of your children may be on a ventilator. Perhaps grief has killed your joy. Your sense of self-worth may be dry and brittle. Your finances could be six feet under. Hopes you held for the future may have passed away long ago.

Can these dead bones live again?

And if so, how?

God promises Ezekiel that he will put flesh and muscles and skin on the bones and breathe life into them, and he makes the same promise to us.

But again, *how*?

What did God tell Ezekiel to do to bring life to the dead bones?

*Speak.*

Not pray, not visualize, not touch, not work. He tells Ezekiel to speak. Just like a mom with a sobbing, stammering toddler, God tells Ezekiel, "Use your words." With those words, the dead "will come to life. Then you will know that I am the LORD" (Ezekiel 37:6 NLT).

Ezekiel had no doubt about what God asked him to do. He didn't respond, "Okay, I'll start praying in my closet," or "I'm just gonna put this as an unspoken on the list of prayer requests," or "I'll get to work on a strategic plan," or "I'll use a positive mindset to envision what I'm hoping will happen."

No.

Ezekiel says, "So I spoke this message, just as he told me" (Ezekiel 37:7).

Ezekiel learned a powerful lesson that day, and it's one we need to embrace as well—speaking words out loud is powerful. Specifically, the words we speak have the power to bring life to our destructive, dry, and dead thoughts.

## WORDS CREATE WORLDS

God could have asked Ezekiel to give quick Swedish massages to each brittle bone. Or told him to think positive thoughts, pray, or write an encouraging note to the dead bones.

But God told Ezekiel to speak. Out loud.

That's how God created the world. He didn't dream it into existence; he *spoke* it into existence. There is power in God's voice.

Three times Jesus brought dead people to life. He healed a dead girl, a dead boy, and a dead friend. How? With a "Young man, I say to you, get up!" and a "My child, get up!" and a "Lazarus, come out!" (Luke 7:14; 8:54; John 11:43).

Speaking words is the tool God has chosen to bring power into the world. God created the world with words. *Your* world was created with words. "The tongue has the power of life and death" (Proverbs 18:21). Proverbs 25:11 reads, "A word fitly spoken is like apples of gold in a setting of silver" (ESV); *The Message* renders it, "The right word at the right time is like a custom-made piece of jewelry."

When I was in the third grade, I remember quite vividly returning from the eye doctor and walking into class wearing glasses for the first time. The thoughts I had in my head were that I looked like a nerd and my classmates were going to laugh when they saw me.

It didn't help that the glasses I had were ridiculous. I looked like a cross between Steve Urkel and Sally Jessy Raphael. When I walked into class, I still remember a couple of the students laughing. Then more students started laughing. I heard the phrase "Nerd Alert" echo across the room. That's when my third-grade teacher Ms. Ziese stopped class and called me to the front. I was horrified as I shuffled to the front with my head down, determined not to cry.

We all thought Ms. Ziese was pretty. Really pretty. She was right out of college and her fiancé was a football player for the local university. As I stood in front of the class, little did I know that my neural pathways of how I would see myself were right then being constructed. Then Ms. Ziese said in front of the entire class, "I see you have some new glasses." As if there was anyone who hadn't noticed. Then she added, "You know, you look like someone to me. Do you know who I think you look like now that you have glasses? I think you look like Clark Kent."

Umm . . . That's *Superman*. And just like that, I went from wanting to disappear to feeling like a nine-year-old superhero. For the rest of the year, I would look in the mirror at my glasses, and could see it. I mean I had to squint, but I *did* look like Superman. A teacher spoke the right word at the right time and, in doing so, gave me words to say to myself.

I asked my friends on social media, "What are some words that have brought life to you over the years." Here are some of their responses:

- "When I grow up, I want to be like you."
- "You're my favorite teacher."
- "I'm praying for you."
- "Kids, doesn't your mom look beautiful tonight?"
- "Good night, Princess."
- "You're a great mommy."
- "You played awesome tonight, Buddy."
- "Your voice is a gift from God."
- "Whoever marries you will be one lucky man."
- "I'm more proud of who you are than what you do."
- "You get prettier every day."
- "You are such a hard worker."

Words also have the power of death. I asked, "What are some words of death that wounded you and are etched in your memory?"

- "That was the worst performance I've seen in twenty-five years of teaching."
- "No one will ever want to be with you. You're damaged goods."
- "You are so lazy."
- "You're just not smart enough."
- "Why can't you be more like your sister?"
- "We're terminating your employment."
- "I wish you had never been born."
- "You will never amount to anything."
- "You and your brother got in the way of me living my life."
- "No one will ever want to marry you."
- "You lost the game for us tonight."
- "I met someone else."

Don't those words just cut to the bone? Proverbs 12:18 reads, "The words of the reckless pierce like swords." And the destructive words of others too often become the words we say to ourselves about ourselves. At the same time, the right words can be life-giving. According to Proverbs 10:11, "The words of the godly are a life-giving fountain" (ESV).

Words are expressions of thought, but they also create and reinforce thoughts. The words we speak, whether we want them to or not, program our subconscious mind. We don't always make the connection because there is time lag between when the seed is planted and the fruit of that seed shows up. But every time we speak, our ears are there to listen, and each word becomes a seed planted in our minds.

Our repeated thoughts create neural pathways. Each thought is like a small axe clearing away branches and making the path more established. But the thoughts we think out loud, that we say with words, are more like a chain saw clearing out that path. Thoughts spoken out loud are especially powerful. The words we speak direct the part of our brains called the reticular activating system (RAS) that notices and gives attention to information confirming or aligning with our verbal assertions. Our words train our brains what to look for and pay attention to.

If we can create worlds with our words, and we can, we need to be a lot more intentional about the words we speak, perhaps especially to ourselves.

I urge you to take three minutes to think about the words you speak to yourself or other people. If the words you speak shape your thoughts, it's good to think about what we say. Look at the two columns of words and circle one word in each row that best describes the words you speak. I'll even give you blank "thinking lines" so you're equipped to set aside this time.

| Angry | Gracious |
|---|---|
| Complaining | Uplifting |
| Harsh | Tender |
| Resentful | Kind |
| Negative | Positive |
| Anxious | Confident |
| Judgmental | Compassionate |
| Gossipy | Blessing |
| Critical | Encouraging |
| Annoyed | Grateful |
| Demanding | Patient |
| Nagging | Inspiring |

# CARELESS WORDS

During my last year of high school, we went on a senior trip to Dallas. A bunch of us were together when we saw someone bungee jumping. Several hundred feet up in the air, this bungee jump was one of the tallest in the country at the time. At least that's how I remember it. We watched as they strapped a cord to some certifiably insane guy's ankles, then the guy dove, headfirst off the platform, plummeted hundreds of feet, and bounced back.

Wanting to appear tough, I blurted out, "I'd do that, but I'm not going to spend forty bucks on it." I guess I wanted everyone to know I was cool enough to bungee jump but too cool to actually spend money on it.

I heard a little commotion behind me, and then one of the girls in my class pulled out a twenty-dollar bill and asked, "Would this help?"

Did I mention that I hate heights? It's definitely a thing. But I hate shame more than heights, so I took the twenty bucks and nervously headed toward the platform.

When I arrived, the guy who was in charge of preserving my life by tying a large rubber band to my ankles did not inspire confidence. He was wearing a 7-Eleven uniform. For real. I was hoping for an aerospace engineer who had spent his life testing and confirming the strength of a bungee cord, but no, this fella's main job was selling Slurpees. Making sure people didn't plunge to their deaths was just a side hustle.

Finally, we were on the platform. I looked down at my friends, and it just seemed so much higher than it had from the ground. I turned to Slurpee Man and said, "I can't do it. I can't do it!"

He said . . . nothing.

I looked back at my friends watching me. I asked him, "Would you give me a shove?"

He said . . . nothing.

I asked again, "Could you just give me a push, sir?"

He said, "Well, we're not legally allowed to push someone off."

"Thank you for being such a rule follower," I responded. "Do you have any other ideas for me?"

He paused. "Well, sometimes it works if you just close your eyes and fall." He added, "Anybody can do that."

*Well,* I thought, *if anybody can do that, I guess I can do that.* So I closed my eyes, and, well, I didn't so much bungee jump; let's say I bungee fell.

It was ~~exhilarating~~ terrifying.

I learned an important lesson that day: Be careful with the words you speak. You let, "I'd do that, but I'm not going to spend forty bucks on it" slip out of your mouth and the next thing you know you're falling two hundred feet.

Jesus warned us about words carelessly spoken in Matthew 12:36–37 (MSG): "Let me tell you something: Every one of these careless words is going to come back to haunt you. There will be a time of Reckoning. Words are powerful; take them seriously. Words can be your salvation. Words can also be your damnation."

Jesus takes very seriously the words we speak, including those we speak not so seriously. He warns us that even our careless words *have the power of life and death.* We need to pay attention to the careless words we speak to others, but also to the careless words we speak to ourselves. It's so easy for the words that have wounded us to become the soundtrack of our lives.

A teacher told you, "You're just not smart enough," and now you tell yourself that every day. She spoke the words, but by repeating them, a neural pathway has been established in your mind. In a moment of frustration, your father said, "You'll never amount to anything," and you've kept that lie as your theme song.

Remember, a lie believed as truth will affect your life as if it were true. Believing the lie, telling it to yourself, gives it power over you. We need to capture those words we so carelessly say to ourselves and replace them with truth.

## SAY IT OUT LOUD

Instead of allowing the power of words to work against us, we're going to take advantage of their power by speaking God's truths over our lives every morning.

I'll explain, but you may be inclined to be skeptical. You've heard the self-empowerment gurus teach about affirming yourself, and you just roll your eyes. I get it, but that's not what this is. I'm not encouraging you to speak your words to yourself, but to speak *God's* word over your life. Now *that* is something that works. You will be taking your thoughts captive and replacing lies with God's truth. As you repeatedly speak God's word out loud to yourself, you will be forming new neural pathways in your brain that will make it easier to automatically think truth instead of lies.

We are going to treat God's word as seed because that's what God tells us to do:

> "The rain and snow come down from the heavens
>> and stay on the ground to water the earth.
> They cause the grain to grow,
>> producing seed for the farmer
>> and bread for the hungry.
> It is the same with my word.
>> I send it out, and it always produces fruit.
> It will accomplish all I want it to,
>> and it will prosper everywhere I send it."

**ISAIAH 55:10–11 NLT**

God's words are like seeds that get planted, seeds that always bear fruit. And that's what we want to do—start planting the seeds of God's words in our minds and in our lives.

Maybe you've been planting some seeds of God's word and the fruit doesn't come right away. You feel like the planting isn't making any difference. I understand the frustration, but you need to remember that this is the way seeds typically work. Farmers plant the seed, and then . . . they wait. Patience is required because fruit is coming.

Every day that we speak words of truth and life, seeds are being planted in our minds. The words are watering the thoughts that will bring life.

# A PARABLE: THE GARDEN OF WORDS

In a distant land, there was a mysterious garden known as the Garden of Words. It wasn't always called that. In fact, how it received the name is quite interesting.

Every person in the nearby village had their own plot in this garden. Some were beautiful with flowers and vegetation; others were overrun with weeds. The people of the village didn't realize that what grew in their gardens was determined by the words they spoke. They didn't know that each word spoken was a seed planted in their garden. Words that were true and kind, excellent and praiseworthy, encouraging and compassionate, became flowers and fruit trees. Negative, harsh, untruthful words were like thorns and weeds.

At the center of each plot stood a fountain called the RAS Watering System. This fountain had an unusual way of watering. It sprinkles whatever plants are most abundant in the garden. If the flowers are flourishing, it waters the flowers. If the weeds are thriving, it waters the weeds, causing them to sprout and grow even more.

One day, a young woman named Lily discovered the secret of the garden. She noticed that her plot, once filled with vibrant flowers, had become overrun with weeds—something the villagers seemed to notice when their children became teenagers. She discovered the mystery of the garden one day as she vented about the mass of weeds that had begun to grow in her plot. She screamed and cursed at herself for having such a horrible garden. And when she was especially letting herself have it, she happened to notice a small sprout appear from the ground. She repeated her words, and yet another weed sprouted up.

She wondered if there might be some connection between the words she spoke and the condition of her garden. She knew one way to find out for sure. "Emily!" she said to herself. Emily was her classmate—the kindest person Lily knew. Lily ran to Emily's plot, and sure enough it was full of flowers and fruit trees.

She decided it was best to keep this secret until she knew for sure. For the next month, Lily was careful about the words she spoke. She purposely started her day speaking words of life and truth. She spoke kind words to others, and even to herself when no one was around. She prayed prayers of thanksgiving and made a list of things she was thankful for. As she got ready in the mornings, she sang worship songs to start the day. After the first week, she couldn't see much difference and was tempted to berate herself for not doing better. Instead, she spoke works of grace and encouragement. Before long she began to see sprouts of beautiful flowers. The RAS Watering System began to shift its water from the weeds to the flowers, and as the flowers grew, the weeds began to disappear.

The people of the village began to call her garden the Garden of Words so that no one would fail ever again to realize the power of their words. The garden became a breathtaking display of color and fragrances—a paradise to which people would come from all around to see and admire.

## EATING YOUR WORDS

We looked at the first part of Proverbs 18:21:"The tongue has the power of life and death." Here's the second part: "And those who love it will eat its fruit." You know the phrase "You're going to have to eat your words"? That's the idea here. Words are like seeds, and whatever seeds we plant will determine the fruit we eat. We may have been speaking poisonous words of death over our lives and eating its fruit. It's time to speak God's words to ourselves, and when we do, these seeds will bear fruit that will change our lives in the best way.

I'll share several examples of what this change might look like. Perhaps you were told the lie that you don't have anything special to offer and will never make a difference. You've been repeating that lie for a long time. But you start waking up and speaking the truth of Ephesians 2:10 over your life: *I am God's masterpiece, and he has prepared good things for me to do, so I will make a difference today.* That's not positive or wishful thinking; it's God's truth, and it's true for your life. You need to speak it so you can think it and then your life will reflect it.

You might tell yourself, day after day, that you are your worst sins, that these sins define you. If you keep saying it, you'll believe it, and you will become a prisoner of your past. How do you break free? By speaking God's truth to yourself from Romans 8:1: *There is no condemnation for me because I am in Christ. The truth is that I've been set free by God's grace, and his grace is enough. So I am going to live free.*

If you've been hurt by other people, it's easy to have a bitter, hard heart toward others and to tell yourself you can't trust anyone. By speaking those words over your life, you take yesterday's pain and bring it into each new day. You can change your life by capturing those thoughts and replacing them with truth based on 2 Corinthians 9:8 and John 1:16: *I am a child of God who has been filled with his grace. I have so much of his grace that I have plenty to give other people.*

If you feel exhausted and keep declaring to yourself, *I'm just too tired; it's all too hard; I can't do this anymore,* you need to choose to stop planting those poisonous seeds and replace them with God's truth from Matthew 11:28–30 and Colossians 1:11: *When I'm tired, I go to Jesus and find rest in him and trust that he will strengthen me with all power so I can endure and be patient.*

You may live each day in fear and anxiety, always worried about what's happening in the world or what might happen in your life. The soundtrack of your life is filled with "what if" and "oh no" lyrics. Because you speak those words, you are living in the negativity of things that have not yet happened and probably never will. What truth should you tell yourself? Here is God's truth based on 1 Peter 5:7: "Today, I am not worried or anxious. That's not who I am. I live above fear because I cast all my cares on God and know that he cares for me."

You might feel alone and tell yourself that no one cares, but God's truth from Hebrews 13:5 says, *I am never alone because I know God will never leave me nor forsake me, and that's the truth I live by.*

It could be that you've been speaking hopeless words over your life. *There's no coming back from this. I was a mess for too long. It's not going to get better.* But you know God's Word, so you know that's not true. You choose to remind yourself of the truth found in Romans 5:4–5 and 1 Corinthians 2:9–12: *God gives me a confident hope that will not disappoint. I have no idea what God has prepared for me because he loves me.*

Again, this isn't humanistic self-empowerment; it's supernatural God-empowerment. This is us speaking God's truth against the lies and into our lives. God created the world with his words, and we are going to recreate our world with his words. God tells us that the words we speak have the power of life and death, so we can and must choose to speak words of life.

## SCIENCE OF SPEAKING

As you repeat God's truth to yourself over and over again (remember, be patient like a farmer), you form new neural pathways. Over time, you will find it easier to think God's thoughts instead of the old self-defeating ones.

It turns out that speaking out loud involves more regions of the brain than if we say the same thing silently to ourselves. Our brains engage in a complex orchestration of activities that involve multiple regions. Silent thoughts have to do with conceptual and linguistic formulation of ideas, but saying them out loud also includes auditory production and perception.

For instance, the part of the frontal lobe called Broca's area is primarily involved in speech production and articulation, and Wernicke's area in the temporal lobe works in understanding spoken and written language. When we say something out loud, both areas work together. The motor cortex part of our brains coordinates our ability to speak and becomes engaged when we say a thought out loud. The auditory cortex processes sound and engages if we speak out loud, but not if we think silently.

It has also been proven that speaking out loud enhances memory retention and recall through the power of the section of our brains known as the hippocampus. The amygdala and ventromedial prefrontal cortex regions, which are involved in emotional processing, are activated when we articulate thoughts or feelings out loud. Why is this significant? Speaking out loud can have a therapeutic effect.

If I lost you in all that brain talk, just know this: It is scientifically proven that it's more powerful to speak out loud. So think out loud by speaking God's truth to yourself—out loud.

## AS I SPOKE

Ezekiel was in a standoff against a valley of dry bones when God told him to speak. Ezekiel, unlike the skeletons he was facing, was all ears: "So I spoke this message, just as he told me."

Then what happened?

> Suddenly as I spoke, there was a rattling noise all across the valley. The bones of each body came together and attached themselves as complete skeletons. Then as I watched, muscles and flesh formed over the bones. Then skin formed to cover their bodies, but they still had no breath in them.
>
> EZEKIEL 37:7-8 NLT

Ezekiel spoke, and it worked. The bones started rattling and coming together. Muscles and flesh and skin formed over the bones.

It was working, but it wasn't enough. They still had "no breath in them." So now what?

> Then he said to me, "Speak a prophetic message to the winds, son of man. Speak a prophetic message and say, 'This is what the Sovereign LORD says: Come, O breath, from the four winds! Breathe into these dead bodies so they may live again.'"
>
> So I spoke the message as he commanded me, and breath came into their bodies. They all came to life and stood up on their feet—a great army.
>
> EZEKIEL 37:9-10 NLT

God tells Ezekiel to speak again. Ezekiel listens to what God said. Then Ezekiel speaks what God said. Then Ezekiel watches what God does. Then Ezekiel listens again to what God said. Then Ezekiel speaks again what God said. Then Ezekiel watches again what God does.

It's going to be the same for us.

We listen to what God says, and then we speak what God just said. Then we do it again. And again. And if we keep saying it out loud, we are going to watch as God does for us what he did for the valley of dead bones.

God brought life to a place of death, and he will do the same for us. He will speak light into our darkness. His word is more powerful than any other word—any word that has been spoken to us or that we've said to ourselves. His word will override all of that if we believe his word and if we say it—again and again—to ourselves.

Do it, and watch what God does.

## CHAPTER 12

# WIN THE MORNING

## STARTING YOUR DAY WITH A PURPOSEFUL PATTERN

"L ife is difficult."

That's the first line of the book *The Road Less Traveled*, which is in the *Guinness Book of World Records* for the most weeks on the *New York Times* bestseller list.[1] The last I heard, it spent 694 weeks on the bestseller list—that's more than thirteen years.[2]

I figured starting this chapter with that line couldn't hurt.

Apparently, people resonate with the idea that life is difficult, and I'm sure you know why. Because . . . life is difficult. There are so many challenges we face. It seems like there's at least one for every day we live, and I wonder if there is one for every letter of the alphabet.

There is.

Check this out and tell me if I'm wrong:

A: Acne

B: Bite people (you know, the person who asks for a bite from your plate at a restaurant)

C: Chewers with their mouths open

D: Driving slow in the passing lane

E: Empty toilet paper roll

F: Food that smells on airplanes

G: Griddle foot injuries (fans of *The Office* understand)

H: Humble braggers

I: In-laws

J: Junk mail

K: Know-it-alls

L: Legos on the floor in the dark

M: Meetings that are pointless

N: "No offense" people

O: One-uppers

P: "Park in two parking spots" people

Q: Quantum physics quizzes

R: "Reply All" emails

S: Slurpers

T: Traffic jams

U: Uber drivers who talk too much

V: Vague social media comments

W: Witty comebacks you didn't think of in time

X: X-press lane that takes forever

Y: Yak attacks

Z: Zoom calls

I did that in a matter of minutes. And while that list is obviously for fun and was also somewhat therapeutic, the truth is that we could come up with another list:

A: Anxiety

B: Bullying

C: Cancer

D: Divorce

E: Eating disorders

F: Financial difficulties

G: Graceless religion

H: Hypocrisy

I: Infertility

J: Job Loss

This is depressing, so I'll stop here. But you get the idea. Life is, in fact, *difficult.*

There is such a torrent of negativity it would be easy to drown in it. Yet we want to live in joy.

That's not just what *we* want; it's God's will for our lives. "Rejoice always, pray continually, give thanks in all circumstances; for this is God's will for you in Christ Jesus" (1 Thessalonians 5:16–18).

We want to rejoice always. For if we don't, we will miss out on God's will, on the abundant life he has for us. We will never become who we are supposed to become.

So, how?

How do we live with joy in a world that hits us with wave after wave of difficulties?

How do we gain victory over the temptations we know will come our way throughout the day?

How do we find the patience to deal with the difficult people we can't avoid?

How do we intentionally fill our minds with thoughts that are true and God honoring?

How do we overcome the voices in our heads that tell us it's too late?

How do we find the energy and strength to be present with the people we care about?

How do we persevere when life seems too difficult?

It starts by *winning the morning*. I can't remember when I first heard the phrase "win the morning." I give credit to my junior high coach who insisted we have our practices before school instead of after. We showed up at practice as the sun rose, and he lined us up for sprints. With William Wallace–like energy, he yelled for us to "win the morning!" Most of us were tolerating the morning at best.

Over time, I discovered much wisdom in these words. The thoughts I think in the morning establish thought patterns that can run through the rest of my day. Taking my thoughts captive and being intentional with my thinking in the morning has a way of setting the course for my day. I wondered if this is just my experience, or if any science can back it up. Is it just me and my fellow morning people, or is it the way God made us?

## SET THE TONE

You may not be a morning person. You may be a little miffed at me mentioning the morning. You may not even be awake enough to believe in God until after lunch.

I get it.

But stay with me.

Your morning may not get started as early as some, but your morning is still the most important part of your day. In fact, your morning sets the course for the rest of your day.

That's not my opinion; it's a fact.

The *Harvard Business Review* found that 92 percent of highly productive people follow planned morning routines.[3] As annoying as these folks may be, they are clearly on to something. Research has shown that a consistent and intentional morning routine can reduce stress and boost energy levels.[4] It can also help lower anxiety.[5] One studied showed that "on average, respondents with a consistent set of morning habits earned roughly $12,500 more per year than those without them." For those more interested in making more love than making more money, more than 75 percent of people with morning routines that included journaling reported having a good sex life.[6]

In a *Forbes* interview, Benjamin Stall and Michael Xander, coauthors of the book *My Morning Routine: How Successful People Start Every Day Inspired*, explain:

> When you have a positive morning in which you're spending your first few hours (or first few minutes, depending on how long you have) doing things that you already decided in advance you really want to do, you're starting your morning with intention. When you start your morning with intention you can bring your morning "wins" with you into the rest of the day.[7]

A morning routine is essential, but not just any morning routine. If you want to set yourself up for a day of distraction and "trigger your stress response" so you are "on edge for the rest of the day," the best morning routine is to check your phone right after you wake up.[8] It's scientifically proven. Explaining why is a little above my pay grade, but it has to do with your brain.

When you wake up, your brain moves from delta waves to theta waves to alpha waves. Important things happen during the theta and alpha wave stages. But if you immediately look at your phone, you skip theta and alpha and jump to a beta state (awake and alert).[9]

If looking at your phone is not the best way to start your day, what should you do?

Steve Jobs had a morning mirror routine. Every morning, he would stare into the mirror and ask himself, *If today were the last day of my life, would I want to do what I am about to do today?* If the answer was no for too many days in a row, he would know he needed to change something in his life.[10]

Marcus Aurelius was intentional with his thoughts to start the day. The Roman emperor started each day with negative visualization. He meditated on the potential challenges of the day and how he would overcome them and face them with virtue.[11]

A number of books trace the morning routines of people like Steve

Jobs and Marcus Aurelius, but it got me wondering what the Bible says about the morning and whether there are any references to how the heroes of our faith started their day:

- Abraham got up early in the morning, split wood for the burnt offering, and set out for a place to worship (Genesis 22:3–5).
- Moses woke up early in the morning to worship and to meet with God (Exodus 24:4; 34:4).
- Gideon rose early in the morning to find the Lord's favor (Judges 6:38; 7:1).
- Hezekiah worshiped God first thing in the morning (2 Chronicles 29:20).
- Job made it his habit to get up early in the morning and sacrifice burnt offerings on behalf of his children (Job 1:5).
- Isaiah spoke of waking up "morning by morning" to listen to God and speak to him (Isaiah 50:4).
- Many psalms point to the morning:
  » Psalm 5:3: "In the morning, LORD, you hear my voice; in the morning I lay my requests before you and wait expectantly."
  » Psalm 59:16: "I will sing of your strength, in the morning I will sing of your love; for you are my fortress, my refuge in times of trouble."
  » Psalm 88:13: "I cry to you for help, LORD; in the morning my prayer comes before you."
  » Psalm 143:8: "Let the morning bring me word of your unfailing love, for I have put my trust in you. Show me the way I should go, for to you I entrust my life."

What about Jesus? "Very early in the morning, while it was still dark, Jesus got up, left the house and went off to a solitary place, where he prayed" (Mark 1:35).

Starting our day by intentionally taking our thoughts captive and setting our minds on what is true, good, lovely, excellent, and praiseworthy is the best way to set the course for our thinking. When we start the day by being transformed by the renewing of our minds, it makes it much less likely that we will be conformed to the patterns of this world as the day continues.

## WIN THE MORNING, AND YOU WIN THE DAY

This is true because of something psychologists call "priming." If you've ever put a coat of primer on a wall before painting it, you know you can't see the primer, but it's there, underneath what you can see. And what you *can* see is different because of what you *can't* see.

Two Dutch researchers conducted a similar experiment by asking a group of students forty-two Trivial Pursuit questions. Before receiving the questions, half of the subjects were asked to take five minutes to think about what life would be like if they were university professors. The other half were asked to spend five minutes thinking about soccer. The soccer group got 42.6 percent of the Trivial Pursuit questions correct; the professor group got 55.6 percent of the Trivial Pursuit questions correct.[12]

The professor group wasn't smarter; they were just primed.

How we start our day primes us for the rest of our day. Our first thoughts set the tone for the thoughts we'll think until we go to sleep at night. If in the morning we prioritize reading the Bible and praying, we are priming our brains with God-thoughts. What happens for the rest of the day? Yes, we will encounter challenges, because life is difficult, but it will be *so much easier* to think God-thoughts. We will have a perspective that is true, noble, right, pure, lovely, admirable, excellent, and praiseworthy.

Our morning sets the tone for our day. Our days become our life.

## LAMENT TO GOD

King Nebuchadnezzar and the armies of Babylon destroyed Jerusalem, but they first surrounded the city so no one could leave and no one could enter to help. Eventually, the people of Jerusalem were starving to death. Even the priests and elders had no food to eat (Lamentations 1:19). People were trading away their treasures for just a bite of food (1:11). Desperate to stay alive, some even resorted to cannibalism (see 4:10, or don't).

Jeremiah was a prophet who had repeatedly warned the people of the consequences if they didn't turn to God, but they hadn't listened. They told him to stop talking so much. And now his dire predictions were becoming their reality.

Jeremiah walks the streets of this once beautiful city, and his heart breaks. He watches as the Israelites rummage through the trash for food. He smells the stench of death. Weeping, he hikes up to a cave overlooking Jerusalem. He wants to pray, but in this moment, he doesn't even know how.

You get it. You may be filled with so much lament that your primary objective each day is to distract yourself. But on those days when you can't help but think about the misery, you don't know how to express what you're going through or how you feel.

Pray? You don't know what to say.

That's Jeremiah. He sits in the cave, not knowing what to say.

Finally he starts with . . . the alphabet. He makes his grievances known to God, one letter at a time. Yep, my listing the bad things in life as an alphabetical acrostic wasn't my idea; I stole it from Jeremiah, who did it about 2,600 years ago in what would become the book of Lamentations.

The Oxford Dictionary defines *lament* as "a passionate expression of grief or sorrow," and that's exactly what Lamentations is—but with a surprise in the middle.

Lamentations is organized in a very intentional way. There are five chapters. Chapters 1, 2, 4, and 5 are each a poem of lament of twenty-two verses. Sandwiched in the middle is chapter 3, in which Jeremiah gives praise and thanks to God.

The book is an illustration of what we're called to do. In the middle of lament, when life seems bookended with sorrow, grief, frustration, and disappointment, we can still be grateful and worship God.

Each of the four chapters of lament are an acrostic of the Hebrew alphabet, which has twenty-two letters. I went through the ABCs one time giving you something wrong in the world for each English language letter; Jeremiah made that trip through the alphabet *four* times.

## EVERY MORNING

In the middle of his lament, Jeremiah pens beautiful words of trust, praise, and worship: "Yet this I call to mind and therefore I have hope" (Lamentations 3:21).

Do you see what Jeremiah is doing? He is taking his thoughts captive. *In spite of everything I see—the difficult circumstances and horrendous situations, this is what I am choosing to think about.* Jeremiah chooses what he will dwell on, and redirecting his thoughts gives him hope.

As Jeremiah begins to choose his thoughts, part of his focus is on the *morning*. He remembers God and his great love and compassion and that they are "new every morning" (Lamentations 3:23). What does Jeremiah do in the morning? He tells himself what is true and good and right about God—"I say to myself" (3:24). If you recall, we learned in the last chapter the importance of what we say to ourselves.

I'll ask again, "What do you say to yourself?"

What do you say to yourself when life isn't going the way you thought it would?

What do you say to yourself when you've got another lonely weekend and everybody else seems to have somebody?

What do you say to yourself when you go to the doctor and find out your cancer is back?

What do you say to yourself when you stumble on some intimate text messages your husband sent to someone you thought was just a friend?

What do you say to yourself when you go in for a routine checkup with the obstetrician and they can't find a heartbeat?

What do you say to yourself when the place you've been working for more than ten years calls you in and says, "We're going in a different direction. Your services are no longer needed"?

What do you say to yourself in those moments when life isn't going the way you hoped it would? What you say to yourself—especially about God—has a way of determining your attitude and behavior, of shaping your relationships and future.

Jeremiah comes into your room before the sun comes up or your alarm goes off. He wakes you up in the early morning to teach you to take your thoughts captive and talk to yourself about God's mercies that are new every morning.

## START, BUT DON'T STAY

Jeremiah begins by being honest with God about his emotions. Remember, taking our thoughts captive begins with our observations about life. Here Jeremiah accuses God of not being fair, and he asks, "Why is this happening, God?"

We get it. When life is bad, it seems like either God is powerful but doesn't care, or he cares but is powerless to do anything about life's difficulties.

A few years back, I pulled into the parking lot of a Best Buy. A storm was approaching, and the wind was already blowing hard. As I got out of my car, the wind blew my door into a new Toyota Camry parked next to me. I saw a pretty big dent, so I left a note with my insurance information. I called my insurance agent and explained what happened. He responded, "Oh. Well, this isn't your fault." I told him, "The owner of the other car was in the store, so I don't think we can pin this on him. I guess it *is* my fault." My insurance guy interrupted me. "No, it's actually called an act of God." I was confused. "So this . . . so this is God's fault then? We just put this one on him?" He laughed and said, "Yes, and it's totally legit. In the insurance industry, we call this an act of God. It's not your fault, not the other guy's fault. It's an act of God."

It seems no matter what their beliefs are about God, a lot of people are pretty comfortable blaming him when life is difficult.

If something goes well, it's "Look what *I* did." But when things go bad, "Look what *God* did." Bad? Act of God. Good? Act of me.

We blame God, which is exactly what Jeremiah does for several verses. He expresses his frustration and disappointment with God:

> He has driven me away and made me walk
> in darkness rather than light;
> indeed, he has turned his hand against me
> again and again, all day long.
>
> He has made my skin and my flesh grow old
> and has broken my bones.
> He has besieged me and surrounded me
> with bitterness and hardship.
> He has made me dwell in darkness
> like those long dead.

LAMENTATIONS 3:2–6

Like Jeremiah, we're tempted to say to ourselves, *Why me? Why is God so mean to me? Why doesn't he make my life better?* We're tempted to start our day feeling sorry for ourselves, focused on things we can't control.

But where do these thoughts take us? Lament has an incredible power to drive us to God *or* drive us away from him. It depends on what we do with these thoughts. They can drive us to despair, discouragement, or depression, or to they can drive us to dependence.

The Bible makes it clear that it's okay to express our pain and grief to God. We can lament. But what we see from the prophet Jeremiah and many of the psalmists is this: *We can start there, but we don't have to stay there.*

We can be honest with God about our feelings and about the situations we wish we could change, but we don't want to stay there. We want to be intentional in reframing our thoughts.

There's a difference between expressing our disappointment and obsessing over it. There's a difference between honestly releasing our frustrations to God and continually rehearsing them.

Jeremiah offers honest laments in chapters 1 and 2, but in chapter 3, he acknowledges where it can lead if we allow ourselves to live in that neural pathway: "I remember my affliction and my wandering, the bitterness and the gall. I well remember them, and my soul is downcast within me" (Lamentations 3:19–20). When we keep track of our disappointments and keep rehearsing them in our minds, a bitter root will start to grow in our hearts that is poisonous. Remembering and repeating the ways we believe that God and other people have let us down leads to discouragement and can contribute to feelings of depression.

Each new morning provides an opportunity to reframe our thoughts around the challenges and troubles we know the day will bring.

A young couple I know went on their honeymoon to a tropical location. After they returned, I ran into the guy and asked, "How was the honeymoon?" He said, "The weather was horrible. We were stuck in our hotel room the whole week. We could've just stayed home and saved all that money." Later I saw the wife and asked, "Hey, how was the honeymoon?" She answered, "It was wonderful. It was just so quiet and restful. We ordered room service. It was so romantic."

I was like, "Hmm, who did you go with? Was it with your husband, or . . . ?" These two people were describing completely different reactions, and yet they had experienced the same situation. What was the difference? They each told themselves a different story.

## THREE THINGS JEREMIAH TELLS HIMSELF

**God's compassions never fail.** This is the first thing Jeremiah says to himself:

> Because of the LORD's great love we are not consumed,
>> for his compassions never fail.
> They are new every morning.
>
> LAMENTATIONS 3:22–23

The word *compassions* conjures up the idea of a mother's womb.

Jeremiah reminds himself that God is mighty and powerful, but at the same time he is tender. A few verses later, Jeremiah writes, "The Master won't ever walk out and fail to return. If he works severely, he also works tenderly" (Lamentations 3:31 MSG).

You may know exactly what this means. Life has been severe, but it has led you to discover a tenderness in God that you couldn't have imagined.

What do you say to yourself when you get out of bed and start your day, even when you know it will be difficult?

*God's compassions never fail. And what's more, they are new every morning.*

Jeremiah affirms that God's mercies are new every morning. *That's* how you win your morning—confident in the never-ending, always fresh compassion of God.

The word *new* here is not like "new of the same kind," but instead "new and of a different kind." It's not, "I had fried eggs for breakfast yesterday; I had new fried eggs for breakfast today." It's more like "I had fried eggs for breakfast yesterday; I had waffles today." New *and* different. When we let God cook, he never serves us leftovers. We can wake up every morning with this in our hearts: "What are we having today, God?" It will be *new*. New mercies. New compassions.

I'm not just asking you to think about what you say to yourself; I'm asking you to think about what you say to yourself specifically *in the morning*. You can say, *This is going to be another long day. I have so much to do that I'll never get it all done. I'll probably disappoint people again.* If you do, you will prime your brain, and it may well be the kind of day you have. You'll look for irritations and find them. Remember, that's how confirmation bias works. We set our thoughts, and then our thoughts look for proof and evidence to support them. Or you can start your morning by reminding yourself of God's new mercies and endless compassions and letting your thoughts look for all the ways you can experience his kindness through the course of the day.

**God's faithfulness is incomparably great.** Jeremiah continues with the second thing he tells himself:

> They [God's compassions] are new every morning;
> great is your faithfulness.

**LAMENTATIONS 3:23**

The truth of the matter is this: Even when we can't see or feel it, God is at work.

You will face challenges and struggles, to be sure. Circumstances can feel overwhelming. It can be hard to have joy and be grateful when there's so much about your life you would change if you could—perhaps when it comes to your health, marriage, children, or vocation. You've prayed prayers, but God doesn't seem to hear or answer them.

How can you rejoice always and give thanks in all circumstances when you feel like you are in a season of lament? By putting your hope, not in your circumstances, but in Jesus. You are counting, not on the situation going the way you want, but on the sovereignty of God. You believe that in all things he can work for good. That he is always faithful to do what he has said he will do. That he is good and is doing good in your life, right now. That his faithfulness will ultimately be demonstrated in full measure on the day Jesus returns and makes everything new.

When we start our day by declaring to God, "Great is your faithfulness," we are saying, *I don't know what's going to happen today. I don't know who will let me down or what I can count on, but one thing I know: I can count on God.*

**The Lord is my portion, and because of that truth, I am content to wait.** The third thing Jeremiah tells himself is this: "The LORD is my portion; therefore I will wait for him" (Lamentations 3:24). Jeremiah's point is that God is enough. He is the only one who can satisfy him. He doesn't need anything else. So he resolves to wait for God.

My favorite Thanksgiving food is my mom's homemade noodles. One year, wonder of wonders, there were some leftovers. Yes! *Praise God from whom all blessings flow.* Later that evening, I went to the fridge, only to discover that my older sister had taken off with all the leftover noodles. *Why, God, why?* I was frustrated and texted her. She responded that she took all the leftover food to a homeless shelter. Great. Just perfect. I now had to pretend that was a good thing to do when inside I was screaming, *Why don't you be generous with your own noodles?*

The next year, my mother made noodles again, but we had thirty people at the house for dinner. I looked at the noodles, counted the people, and concluded there were not enough portions. When no one was looking, I secretly put some noodles in a bowl before the meal started and hid it in the back of the refrigerator.

Everyone ate dinner, watched football, and played Ping-Pong, but the whole time, I was thinking about my noodles. My portion was set aside, and I was waiting for it. I had to wait for everyone to leave and for my wife to fall asleep. The time finally came, and my portion was there. I had waited for it . . . and it was ready . . . and it was good.

Jeremiah tells us that God is kind of like my mom's noodles—so worth waiting for. He is writing to people who are starving to death, trading their treasures for a bite of food. But in essence, Jeremiah tells them, "It's hard now, but the Lord is still our portion. We will wait for him."

When life is difficult, what do you say to yourself?

Who or what is your portion?

You may think, *If I can just get married, then I'll be happy. I am waiting on a spouse.* Or *I will wait on a child.* Or *I will wait on an inheritance.* Or *I am waiting on a promotion. When I get that thing I'm waiting for, well, then I'll be satisfied.* No, you won't. The Lord is your portion. He is the only one who is enough.

Charles Spurgeon preached to people who have experienced loss about this passage in Lamentations:

> You have lost much, Christian, but you have not lost your portion. Your God is your all; therefore, if you have lost all but God, still you have your all left, since God is all. The text does not say that God is only part of our portion but the whole portion. . . . [Imagine that] It is daylight and the sun is shining bright, and I have a candle lit, but someone blows it out. Shall I sit me down and weep, because my candle has been

extinguished? Nay, not while the sun shines. If God be my portion, if I lose some little earthly comfort—I will not complain, for heavenly comfort remains.[13]

Someone or something can come and blow out our candles, but the sun is still shining. In the middle of our lament, we have reason to be thankful and grateful.

And that's not an easy attitude to maintain because life is undeniably difficult. There's no way to do it without taking our thoughts captive. And how do we do that? With a "Yet this I call to mind" and a "I say to myself," we win the morning.

## CHAPTER 13

# ON THINGS ABOVE

## SETTING YOUR MIND ON ETERNITY

I t happened at a Pizza Hut. I asked my girlfriend's father if I could have her hand in marriage, promising him I'd be a good husband.

Adoniram Judson asked his girlfriend's father if he could have her hand in marriage, promising him she would likely die a violent death.

Kind of different.

Adoniram Judson was about to become one of America's first foreign missionaries. As a twenty-four-year-old in the early 1800s, he set sail for India and ended up in Burma. He had fallen in love with Ann and wanted to marry her, but only if she were willing to go with him to a part of the world that would be difficult and hostile.

Adoniram sent Ann's father a letter asking for his permission. Here is a portion of that letter:

> I have now to ask, whether you can consent to part with your daughter
> early next spring, to see her no more in this world? Whether you can

consent to her departure to a heathen land, and her subjection to the hardships and sufferings of a missionary life? Whether you can consent to her exposure to the dangers of the ocean; to the fatal influence of the southern climate of India; to every kind of want and distress; to degradation, insult, persecution, and perhaps a violent death?

Can you consent to all this, for the sake of Him who left His heavenly home and died for her and for you; for the sake of perishing, immortal souls; for the sake of Zion and the glory of God? Can you consent to all this, in hope of soon meeting your daughter in the world of glory, with a crown of righteousness brightened by the acclamations of praise which shall redound to her Savior from heathens saved, through her means, from eternal woe and despair?[1]

If you're the father, what do you say to that?

He responded by essentially saying, "She can make up her own mind."

In 1813, Adoniram and Ann were married and set sail to Burma, where they experienced one hardship after another. That letter was more prophetic than he could have known.

In 1824, Adoniram was put in prison. While in prison he wasted away, becoming unrecognizable and nearly crippled from the torture. At night, the jailors would tie Adoniram's feet together, then the jailer would hoist his feet into the air so only the back of his shoulders and head would be resting on the ground. That's how he would sleep—often with temperatures over 110 and with mosquitoes eating him alive.

While in prison Adoniram found out his wife was expecting. Pregnant Ann would walk two miles to the jail every day to plead for her husband's release, but her wish was not granted. Adoniram spent eighteen months in prison.

Baby Maria was born, and Ann became sick which led to her milk drying up.

The jailer eventually had mercy on the Judsons and let Adoniram out of prison each evening for a couple hours so he could take their baby into a nearby village and beg for other nursing mothers to nurse his baby.

Finally, Adoniram was released from prison. It was just in time to watch his wife die. Six months later his daughter, Maria, died as well.

Adoniram eventually remarried. His second wife also died on the mission field. He would bury seven children in Burma before he died at age sixty-one.

When you hear the story, you instinctively feel sorry for them.

Here's my question: Should we?

Should we feel sorry for them, or should we feel sorry for us?

We'll return to that question, but first I want us to fix our minds on things above.

## SPOILER ALERT

I hope this doesn't ruin the ending for you, but . . . you are going to die.

In his book *The Denial of Death*, Ernest Becker makes the case that if there's one thing we don't like to think about, it's death. Becker argues that much of human behavior is driven by our attempts to ignore or avoid the reality of our mortality, to suppress the most irrefutable fact in the whole world—I am going to die.[2]

We don't like talking about death so much that we've created ways to say it without saying it. We tell our friends that someone "passed away," "went to the other side," or "went on ahead of us." If we are feeling a little less formal, we might say they "kicked the bucket," "bought the farm," "are pushing up daisies," or "are swimming with the fishes."

We invented all these ways to say death without saying death because death seems so final. But it's *not*. And unless we think about death, we won't rightly be able to think about life.

Death is just a door. This life is preparation for the next, and death is how you pass from one to the other.

Avoided thinking about death has made us think mostly about this life on earth. Even as you've been challenged in this book to think about your thoughts, my guess is that all of your attention has been focused on your life *before death*. But that's not a particularly wise way to think about our existence.

James 4:14 asks, "What is your life? You are a mist that appears for a little while and then vanishes." Now that I think of it, this would be a good thought exercise. Walk into the kitchen or bathroom, wherever you keep the Febreze or the Poo-Pourri (a real thing), and pump a few sprays into the air. You can even hold that trigger down for a whole minute. Then watch how quickly it disappears. James says your life is like that. So why are you spending all your time and energy thinking about the mist and not taking time to think about eternity?

Thinking about eternity is like the top button on a dress shirt. If we focus on the top button and pay attention to lining it up with the right hole, all the other buttons will line up without having to think about them. But if we aren't paying attention to the top button, none of the other buttons will line up the way they should. As we intentionally think about eternity, many of our other thoughts around everything else will line up correctly.

The thought patterns of this world are all focused on what's happening in this world. An eternal thought pattern is external to the visible world. It helps us think rightly about the circumstances making us anxious, the relationship making us insecure, the screen screaming for our attention, the state of our finances that have us in despair, and the pleasure of the moment we're tempted to live for.

Whether we die at forty or eighty, our time on earth is short in comparison to our entire existence. After we spend fifty thousand years in heaven, if we were to look back at our life on earth, it would be like one-tenth of 1 percent of our existence. I didn't do the math on that, but you get what I'm saying. When someone dies at forty, we view it as tragic, and yet I assume from the perspective of eternity that our lives on earth will seem vapor short, no matter how long they lasted. I suspect in heaven the difference between dying at forty and dying at eighty would be like the difference between having a reservation at 5:00 p.m. and not being seated until 5:10. In that light, Moses prayed with great wisdom, "Teach us to number our days, that we may gain a heart of wisdom" (Psalm 90:12).

A while back, I came across a website called Death Clock. All you need to do is enter some information, and it gives an estimated date of death. I used it once for an illustration in a teaching and then decided to do it again and . . . somehow I lost nine years! I don't know what I'm doing differently, but my new date of death is May 11, 2065.

The website has a clock that counts down in seconds. I can actually see how many seconds I have left, but of course, there are no money-back guarantees. It might be nice if we knew for sure and could truly number our days, but we can't. We just know the end is coming, and therefore we should live with the end in mind.

We've been thinking about our thinking, which is what the apostle Paul encourages us to do—not think so much about *now* and instead focus on *what comes next*. And as we think about what comes next, we'll have the right thoughts about what's happening now:

> Set your minds on things above, not on earthly things. For you died, and your life is now hidden with Christ in God. When Christ, who is your life, appears, then you also will appear with him in glory.
>
> COLOSSIANS 3:2–4

## THE END IN MIND

Considering how short this life is and how long the next life is, the only thing that makes sense is to *live with the end in mind*. Think eternity.

Most of us don't. It's easy not to.

Jesus told a story about a man so focused on this life that he ignored the next one. Luke 12 depicts Jesus teaching and helping people to look at life through the lens of eternity. He explains that we should not fear people who have the power to kill us, but to instead "fear him who, after your body has been killed, has authority to throw you into hell" (Luke 12:5).

Someone in the crowd interrupts Jesus' teaching on eternity with a question: "Teacher, tell my brother to divide the inheritance with me" (Luke 12:13). While Jesus is teaching about eternity, this man's question focuses on something extremely temporary.

Jesus turns to the crowd and tells them a parable:

> "The ground of a certain rich man yielded an abundant harvest. He thought to himself, 'What shall I do? I have no place to store my crops.'
>
> "Then he said, 'This is what I'll do. I will tear down my barns and build bigger ones, and there I will store my surplus grain. And I'll say to myself, "You have plenty of grain laid up for many years. Take life easy; eat, drink and be merry."'
>
> "But God said to him, 'You fool! This very night your life will be demanded from you. Then who will get what you have prepared for yourself?'
>
> "This is how it will be with whoever stores up things for themselves but is not rich toward God."
>
> LUKE 12:16–21

This guy is having conversations with himself about what to do with all his wealth. His thoughts are simply consumed with what he's going to do with all his extra bounty.

In this chat he's having with his favorite person, he refers to himself nine times in just two verses. He speaks of "my crops," "my barns," "my grain," and "my goods." He is focused on himself. He's also laser focused on the temporary. There is no thought of what might come next—it's all about his temporary pleasure and comforts.

Then God calls him a name. It seems to me it's the worst name God can call a person. He says this man is a *fool*.

Why?

Because he isn't living with the end in mind. His death clock starts ticking. It's time for him to pass from his sixty-year life on earth into his sixty-million-year life in eternity, but he hasn't spent any time thinking about or preparing for forever. In God's book, that makes you a fool.

The man in Jesus' parable gave no thought to his eternal destination. He *was* planning for the future, but only the future of *this* life. I'm sure he was known as a strategic thinker, but he only thought strategically about the mist. He built bigger barns, thinking, *Now I'll be ready for whatever comes my way*, but Jesus says he was a fool because he wasn't ready for death. He was a fool because he thought long-term, but not long-term enough. He was focused on the next thirty years, but what about the next thirty billion?

Stop for a minute and think about how much you think about eternity. Your answer to that question reveals whether or not you're a fool.

After telling the parable, Jesus said to his disciples, "Therefore I tell you, do not worry about your life, what you will eat; or about your body, what you will wear" (Luke 12:22). As we take our thoughts captive, we need to think past the pay raise, the dream house, the nice vacation, the relaxing retirement and think about what comes after the things we think so much about.

Don't worry about our lives? Okay, what should we do instead? "Sell your possessions and give to the poor. Provide purses for yourselves that will not wear out, a treasure in heaven that will never fail, where no thief comes near and no moth destroys" (Luke 12:33).

Do you live with the end in mind? If you look at your relationships, finances, calendar—how you spend your time and energy—would all of it say that you are using this life to prepare for your next life?

We need to set our minds on things above, not on earthly things.

## LAST WORDS

Someday you and I will speak the last words of our lives here on earth. What will your last words be?

The apostle Paul's last letter was written to his ministry apprentice Timothy. Paul doesn't have much time left here on earth. According to the historian Eusebius, Paul would soon be headed for execution under the reign of Emperor Nero. Paul knows a brutal execution awaits him as he writes the words we now have as the book of 2 Timothy.

> For I am already being poured out like a drink offering, and the time for my departure is near. I have fought the good fight, I have finished the race, I have kept the faith. Now there is in store for me the crown of righteousness, which the Lord, the righteous Judge, will award to me on that day—and not only to me, but also to all who have longed for his appearing.
>
> 2 TIMOTHY 4:6-8

## A DRINK OFFERING

Paul says he was "being poured out like a drink offering"—a phrase that doesn't mean much to us. When we read the word *drink*, we might think of Kool-Aid or Arnold Palmers. When Timothy read this letter, he knew Paul was referring to the Old Testament sacrificial system in which a drink offering was the least impressive, the humblest offering a person could give to God. When Paul describes his life that way, he is saying, "I may not be impressive, but I have poured my life out on the altar of God. I have given everything I am."

You and I are pouring our lives out on the altar of something. The question is, What are we giving our lives to?

As a pastor, I've officiated countless funerals, sometimes for people I've never met. I always meet with the family to learn details of the person's life that I can share in the service. I ask, "Would you help me get to know them? What were they passionate about? What did they live for?"

One of the first times I asked that question was as I prepared for the funeral of a young man in his thirties who had died in an accident. My question was followed by silence. Everyone looked around, hoping someone else might have something worthwhile to say. Finally, his mom broke the silence, "Well, my son loved hats."

I asked, "Like baseball caps?"

"Oh," his mother seemed relieved to add a few words, "any kind of hats."

I smiled. "So he loved hats. What else might you tell me?"

More silence.

Followed by more silence.

His mother spoke up again. "You need to come by and see his hat collection sometime."

And everyone else in the room began to chime in with more details about his different hats.

I've had a lot of these kinds of conversations. And I will say that it's not any less sad to me when it's a car collection instead of a hat collection.

Sometimes people will say something like, "Oh, he was a huge sports fan" or "She loved to decorate." Okay, I get it. That's fine, it's good to have a hobby, but what else? Please tell me there's something else.

"He loved golf."

"She loved romance novels."

"She never missed an episode of *The Young and the Restless*."

I will tell you what I want to say in those solemn sessions but never have: "She lived an entire life, and we're talking about a soap opera?" "Just to be clear, we are talking about the summation of a man's life, and we're discussing golf?"

In those moments I also feel very convicted and realize how little time I spend thinking about eternity and asking questions like, *What would my family and friends say about me?*

I invite you to take a few moments and close your eyes and picture a small room at a funeral home? Imagine I'm sitting there with maybe three to seven chairs around me, each filled with a family member or friend of yours. I ask, "Tell me about your loved one. What were they like?" "What were they passionate about?" "What did they live for?"

Go around that circle of chairs, picturing these people from your life. What do you think they would say? What altar are you pouring your life onto?

I'll give you several blank lines to think about this. But don't just think about it for three minutes; think about it a lot. Set your mind on it.

## MY DEPARTURE

Paul's next sentence in his letter to Timothy helps us understand death: "The time for my departure is near." One of the ways to translate *depart* is "set sail."

Paul is speaking of his death, but the word he uses does not mean an "end"; it actually connotes a "beginning." Paul isn't kicking the bucket or buying the farm; he is setting sail. Death is not an ending, but rather a departure—it's the new beginning of the great next. When we begin to think of it this way, it changes how we think about everything else.

Paul isn't dreading death; he is anticipating it. He wrote in Philippians 1:21, "For to me, to live is Christ and to die is gain." Living is good, but dying is better. Living allows me to continue living for God, but dying means I get to be with him in a new and more complete way. He continues, "I desire to depart and be with Christ, which is better by far; but it is more necessary for you that I remain in the body" (Philippians 1:23–24).

Because of Jesus, thinking about eternity is not something we carry out with dread and fear. Instead, we think of heaven in a way that gives us hope, joy, and peace. The more we set our minds on things above, the more the neural pathways get established and the more our anticipation and longing begin to build.

One of the reasons it can be difficult to think about heaven is that we have trouble picturing it. Have you ever anticipated going on a long-awaited vacation? What do you do? You pull up pictures of the resort. You watch YouTube videos of where you'll be visiting. You take a picture off the internet that captures the view from the balcony and make it your screen saver. You go to Tripadvisor and think about the great restaurants you want to eat at or the fascinating excursions you want to take. Your research helps you think about what it's going to be like, and your anticipation builds. In fact, just thinking about these pictures and watching these videos activates your brain's reward system and releases dopamine, the neurotransmitter associated with pleasure. This is why life is better when you have a vacation on the calendar.

We may try to think like this about heaven, but we have trouble picturing it. Quoting Isaiah 64:4, Paul wrote in 1 Corinthians 2:9 (NLT), "No eye has seen, no ear has heard, and no mind has imagined what God has prepared for those who love him."

Even though our minds can't conceive it, how about we take a few minutes to think about it?

People worry that in heaven we will lose the physical pleasures of earth, but God created those physical pleasures. I believe what we experience now is just a sampling—like when we go to the ice cream shop, and they give us a taste. The most satisfying pleasures of this life are merely a sample of what we will experience in heaven.

Heaven will be a place of incredible beauty. John tells us that heaven has been "prepared as a bride beautifully dressed for her husband" (Revelation 21:2). The streets, walls, and gates are said to be made of valuable jewels. Heaven will be the ultimate for beautiful scenery and breathtaking creation. The same God who created the most beautiful parts of this world is preparing a place for you. The national parks and seven wonders of the world are just previews of coming attractions. After all, it's the same architect.

Revelation 21 describes heaven as a city that is fifteen hundred miles cubed. That means it goes upward too, like 780,000 stories high! For those who prefer rural settings to metropolitan areas, don't worry, there's a place for you. Revelation says we'll be able to go in and out of the city. There will be plenty of exploring to do. Revelation 6 and 19 portray horses in heaven. While other animals aren't mentioned, it seems likely that other animals will be there too. Isaiah 11 speaks of wolves, lions, and lambs in the new earth. So imagine going for a hike in heaven and seeing lions and bears and, who knows, maybe dinosaurs and new species as well.

Here's part of what makes heaven so beautiful: "The city does not need the sun or the moon to shine on it, for the glory of God gives it light, and the Lamb is its lamp" (Revelation 21:23). I honestly don't know exactly how that will work, but I can't wait to experience it.

Heaven is also a place of delightful rest—and how we need that. We race through life busy and burdened. When people ask us how we're doing, we say, "I'm tired. I just have a lot going on." We need rest, and God promises it. "'Blessed are the dead who die in the Lord from now on. 'Yes,' says the Spirit, 'they will rest from their labor, for their deeds will follow them'" (Revelation 14:13). Think about what it will be like with an eternity of no stress, no pressure, no bills, no deadlines—just perfect rest.

Some people worry that heaven will be boring and unproductive, that around the year 4973 they'll get bored of lounging around on cloud futons. An emphatic no! Heaven will be a place of meaningful service: "The throne of God and of the Lamb will be in the city, and his servants will serve him" (Revelation 22:3).

Heaven will be a place of loving relationships. Think of the joy of being reunited with parents, children, grandparents, and Christian friends who have preceded us in death. We may have more loved ones in heaven than we do on earth. We'll not only be reunited with loved ones, but we will form new friendships as well. In Matthew 8, Jesus speaks of sitting down in heaven and eating with Abraham, Issac, and Jacob. Think about that. I can't wait to hear Adam describe what he first thought when he saw Eve. Or listen to Noah tell the story of what it was like to be on the ark. Or listen to Mary tell stories about Jesus when he was growing up. And it's not just inspiring people from Scripture I can't wait to meet. What will it be like to go on a hike with C. S. Lewis, have coffee with Harriet Tubman, shoot baskets with Pete Maravich, or go exploring with Jim Elliot.

Heaven will be a place of uninhibited worship:

> Then I heard what sounded like a great multitude, like the roar of rushing waters and like loud peals of thunder, shouting:
>
> > Hallelujah!
> > > For our Lord God Almighty reigns.
> > Let us rejoice and be glad
> > > and give him glory!
>
> REVELATION 19:6–7

I hate to disappoint, but we won't be lounging around listening to cherubs gently play their harps. We will join in, and our worship will be like the roar of rushing water and loud peals of thunder.

Why will we worship God like never before? Because we will know him like never before:

> For now we see only a reflection as in a mirror; then we shall see face to face. Now I know in part; then I shall know fully, even as I am fully known.
>
> 1 CORINTHIANS 13:12

That's the highlight of heaven—we will see God face-to-face and know him in a way we've longed for but have never had.

In some of his last words on earth, Paul tells Timothy, "The time for my departure has come," and *that's* what he was departing for—of course dying was gain!

Paul was fixated on his departure because he couldn't wait to get where he was going. It's often not quite the same for us. Imagine setting off on a weekend getaway but when you arrive, you're not thrilled with your hotel room. The carpet has a tear in it. Some of the wallpaper is peeling off. It's got that popcorn ceiling. You were hoping it would have a mini fridge, but no such luck. Then you lie down on the bed and . . . uncomfortable mattress. Ugh.

You think, *I'm going to be here for the entire weekend, so I'm gonna fix the place up.* Once you start, you get into it and think to yourself, *I'm going to do this right.* You hire a team of workers to tear out the carpet, peel the wallpaper off the walls, scrape the popcorn off the ceiling, and remove the bed. You dig into your savings account to have a mahogany wood floor put in, a top-of-the-line full-size refrigerator, and one of those Sleep Number smart beds. You are now out of money, but once you find out that the TV in the room isn't as smart as your TV at home, you order a 75-inch flat screen with your credit card.

Finally, at the end of your second day, everything is just the way you want it. You lie down in your new bed, look around, sigh, and say to yourself, *So worth it.* The next morning, you wake up to a text message reminding you that your checkout time is at 11:00 a.m.

I'm sure you would agree, but this is an insane scenario. Yet this is exactly how we live when we don't think about eternity. We give all our time, energy, and money to the mist of our life here that appears for a moment and then vanishes, while ignoring the life we will live forever.

## FINISHED

Paul continues in his last letter, "I have finished the race, I have kept the faith." Keeping his mind on things above gave him strength to finish strong.

Earlier, I told you the harrowing story of Adoniram and Ann Judson and asked, *Should we feel sorry for them, or should we feel sorry for us?*

We feel sorry for *them*, right? Imprisoned. Tortured. Death. Kids dying. It just doesn't make sense . . . unless we look at it through the lens of eternity. If this life is just a mist, then what they did makes a lot of sense.

That's how Ann looked at it. She knew what she was getting into and *chose* it. When she was processing the decision of whether or not to go, she wrote a letter to her best friend, Lydia Kimble:

> I feel willing and expect, if nothing in providence prevents, to spend my days in this world in heathen lands. Yes, Lydia, I have about come to the determination to give up all my comforts and enjoyments here, sacrifice my affection to relatives and friends, and go where God, in his providence, shall see fit to place me.[3]

She chose to give up her comforts and enjoyments. When she said yes, she knew she was likely saying goodbye to her family and friends forever.

We can feel sorry for her, but she didn't feel sorry for herself. And I wonder if she might feel sorry for us.

We get so caught up in the temporary trappings of this world that we miss out on living for what matters and will last forever. Jesus said, "Everyone who has left houses or brothers or sisters or father or mother or wife or children or fields for my sake will receive a hundred times as much and will inherit eternal life" (Matthew 19:29).

What are we missing out on when we don't set our minds on things above?

In light of eternity, Ann Judson did not regret the way she chose to invest her life. It's always the right choice when we live now with forever in mind.

What came of the Judsons' decision to move to Burma? Adoniram faced nearly four decades of opposition and suffering. But all of that was temporary. Here's what wasn't temporary: Adoniram translated the entire Bible into Burmese. And yes, he outlived seven of his children, but when he died there were *more than seven thousand* children of God in Burma because he had brought the gospel to them.

Today there are more than 3,700 churches that trace their beginning back to the day Adoniram and Ann decided to set sail. In fact, some years ago, I told the story of the Judsons in a sermon. After the service, three young men came over to introduce themselves. They were in America doing mission work. They were from Burma. They were Burmese missionaries to America. All three had become Christians at the same church in Burma. The name of that church? Judson Church.

Our lives will change when we change the way we think, and there is nothing we should think about more than the things above.

## FINAL THOUGHTS

We began this book by acknowledging a universal truth—our minds are being molded. Every day, we face an onslaught of thoughts that threaten to conform us to the patterns of this world—patterns of insecurity, distraction, offense, misplaced pleasure, and despair. We've seen how these thought patterns can shape our emotions, drive our actions, and ultimately determine the course of our lives.

But we've also discovered this incredible promise: We are not helpless victims of our thoughts. Through the power of Christ and the renewal of our minds, we can break free from destructive thought patterns and experience true transformation.

Hear me say it again, this isn't just positive thinking or self-help strategies; it's partnering with God in the process of rewiring our brains. It's about taking every thought captive and making it obedient to Christ. It's about allowing the truth of God's Word to reshape our neural pathways and redefine our reality.

The challenge before us is great, but so is the promise. Imagine a life in which our thoughts no longer hold us captive, but instead propel us toward God's purpose for our lives. Imagine habits broken, relationships restored, emotions healed, purpose discovered, and peace that transcends understanding becoming our daily reality.

So, what's the next step?

1. Choose one thought pattern to focus on. Is it insecurity? Distraction? The tendency to take offense? Whatever it is, acknowledge it before God.
2. Begin the practice of taking these thoughts captive. Use the strategies we've discussed—intentional input exposure, Scripture meditation, prayer, thought-stopping techniques. Remember, this is a skill that improves with practice.
3. Surround yourself with truth tellers. Find a community that will remind you of God's truth when you've forgotten it.
4. Be patient with yourself. Neural pathways aren't rewired overnight. Celebrate small victories and keep pressing forward.
5. Stay connected to the source. All of your efforts at mind renewal will be futile if you're not continually connecting to Christ, the author and perfecter of your faith.

As you step into this journey of mind renewal, know that you're not alone. The God who began a good work in you is faithful to complete it. He is for you, not against you. And he delights in transforming you from the inside out.

The battle for your mind is real, but victory is assured in Christ. The journey of a thousand miles begins with a single step or, in this case, a single thought. What will yours be?

# APPENDIX

## HOW TO KEEP A THOUGHT JOURNAL

A s this book comes to an end, I want to invite you to keep a thought journal. Why? Because taking your thoughts captive begins with understanding the power of your thoughts and taking the time to think about what you have been thinking about.

Imagine for a moment that your mind is a vast library, filled with shelves upon shelves of thoughts. Some are dusty old thoughts that have been handed down from one generation to the next. You're not sure how you got them; they've just always been on the shelves. Others are flashy new arrivals, the latest and most popular thoughts demanding your attention. Some are trashy paperbacks you're not quite sure how you acquired, and you're embarrassed you have them, but there they are.

Now picture yourself as the librarian of this thought collection. When was the last time you took inventory of your thoughts? Have you ever paused to examine what is occupying the prime real estate of your mind?

This is where a thought journal comes in. We need to intentionally examine the thoughts we allow in the library of our brains, because they are shaping everything about us. And we can't take our thoughts captive if we don't know what thoughts we're thinking.

Below is an exercise to help you keep a thought journal. If you will be honestly and courageously aware of your thought patterns, you can begin to be made new in the attitudes of your mind. Take a deep breath. Grab your mental clipboard. It's time to start your thought journal and discover what's really on your mind.

## STEP 1: THOUGHT CAPTURE

- Choose three times during the day when you will pay attention to your thoughts.
  - » Examples: waking up / taking a shower / driving to work / going to bed / scrolling on social media
- Take three minutes to write down your thoughts in a small notebook or in your Notes app on your phone.
- Identify and write down the trigger for each thought you have. It should look something like this:
  - » Time: early morning
  - » Thought: overwhelmed by all I have to do today
  - » Trigger: calendar alert on my phone

## STEP 2: THOUGHT CLASSIFICATION

- Review your captured thoughts.
- Categorize as positive, negative, or neutral.
- See if there is a pattern.
- It should look something like this:
  - » Thought: so much to do today
  - » Category: negative
  - » Theme: morning pressure

# STEP 3: THOUGHT CONNECTION

- Connect your thought to an emotion.
- Rate the emotional impact of the thought on a scale of 1 to 10 based on frequency and intensity. How common is the emotion and how long does it tend to last?
- It should look something like this:
  » Thought: so much to do today / negative
  » Emotion: anxious and irritated
  » Scale: 6

# STEP 4: THOUGHT CHECK

- Check your thought by asking questions.
  » How true is this thought on a scale of 1 to 10?
  » What is the biblical perspective on this thought?
- It should look something like this:
  » Thought: too much to do
  » Truth scale: 3
  » Biblical perspective: 1 Peter 5:7: "Cast all your anxiety on [God] because he cares for you."

# STEP 5: THOUGHT TRANSFORMATION

- Reframe your thought in a way that is intentional and renewed.
- Example: "I have a lot to do today, but God knows, and he will give me the strength and grace I need along the way."

## Chapter 1: Mind Molding

1. Dallas Willard, "For Such a Time as This: Part 6: Living Without Hurry and Worry," YouTube, May 22, 2021, www.youtube.com/watch?v=ta_A1Po-xaE.

2. See Caroline Leaf, "Take Your Thoughts Captive . . . Here's How," Preach It Teach It, December 31, 2018, https://preachitteachit.org/articles/take -your-thoughts-captive-heres-how/amp/. Note that research on how many thoughts we think each day isn't an exact science. For example, a 2020 study suggested that "people typically have more than 6,000 thoughts per day": see Crystal Raypole, "How Many Thoughts Do You Have Each Day? And Other Things to Think About," Healthline, February 28, 2022, www .healthline.com/health/how-many-thoughts-per-day.

3. Jonathan Haidt, *The Happiness Hypothesis: Finding Modern Truth in Ancient Wisdom* (New York: Basic Books, 2006), 1–5, 13–17.

4. Margarit Brigham, "Breaking 80 with Visualizations and Belief," Golf State of Mind, April 29, 2011, https://golfstateofmind.com/breaking-80-with -visualizations-and-belief/.

## Chapter 2: The Law of Cognition

1. Donald L. Unger, "Does Knuckle Cracking Lead to Arthritis of the Fingers?," *Arthritis and Rheumatism* 41, no. 5 (1998): 949–50, https://pubmed.ncbi .nlm.nih.gov/9588755/; see also Steve Mirsky, "Crack Research: Good News About Knuckle Cracking," *Scientific American*, December 1, 2009, www .scientificamerican.com/article/crack-research/.

2. Robert L. Swezey and Stuart E. Swezey, "The Consequences of Habitual Knuckle Cracking," *Western Journal of Medicine* 122 (1975): 377–79, www .ncbi.nlm.nih.gov/pmc/articles/PMC1129752/pdf/westjmed00297-0049.pdf.

3. See David E. Rumelhart, "Schemata: The Building Blocks of Cognition," in *Theoretical Issues in Reading Comprehension*, ed. Rand J. Spiro et al. (New York: Routledge, 1980), 33–58.

## Chapter 3: The Rule of Exposure

1. Brian Koppelman, "Seth Goodin 1/1/19," *The Moment* podcast, January 1, 2019, 50:43, www.podcast24.fi/episodes/the-moment-with-brian -koppelman/seth-godin-1-1-19.

2. "What Seth Godin Said About *See You at the Top*," *This Is Broken*, accessed November 12, 2024, www.thisisbroken.co.uk/books/see-you-at-the-top/.

3. Cited on Seth Godin's website, www.sethgodin.com.

4. See Charlotte Nickerson, "Mere Exposure Effect in Psychology: Biases and Heuristics," Simply Psychology, updated October 10, 2023, www .simplypsychology.org/mere-exposure-effect.html.

5. Rebecca L. Collins et al., "Watching Television Predicts Adolescent Initiation of Sexual Behavior," *Pediatrics* 114, no. 3 (2004): 280–89.

6. L. Rowell Huesmann et al., "Longitudinal Relations Between Children's Exposure to TV Violence and Their Aggressive and Violent Behavior in Young Adulthood: 1977–1992," *Developmental Psychology* 39, no. 2 (2003): 201–21, www.apa.org/pubs/journals/releases/dev-392201.pdf.

7. Gráinne M. Fitzsimons et al., "Automatic Effects of Brand Exposure on Motivated Behavior: How Apple Makes You 'Think Different,'" *Journal of Consumer Research* 35, no. 1 (2008): 21–35, https://academic.oup.com/jcr /article-abstract/35/1/21/1847975?redirectedFrom=fulltext.

8. Paul J. Wright et al., "A Meta-Analysis of Pornography Consumption and Actual Acts of Sexual Aggression in General Population Studies," *Journal of Communication* 66, no. 1 (2016): 183–205, https://academic.oup.com/joc /article-abstract/66/1/183/4082427?redirectedFrom=fulltext.

9. Dale Kunkel and Brian L. Wilcox, "Children and Media Policy: Historical Perspectives and Current Practices," in *Handbook of Children and the Media*, 2nd ed., ed. Dorothy G. Singer and Jerome L. Singer (Los Angeles: Sage, 2011), 569–94.

10. Pilar Aparicio-Martinez et al., "Social Media, Thin-Ideal, Body Dissatisfaction and Disordered Eating Attitudes: An Exploratory Analysis," *International Journal of Environmental Research and Public Health* 16, no. 21 (2019): 4177, https://pmc.ncbi.nlm.nih.gov/articles/PMC6861923/.

11. E. Alison Holman et al., "Media Exposure to Collective Trauma, Mental Health, and Functioning: Does It Matter What You See?" *Clinical Psychological Science* 8, no. 1 (2019): 111–24, https://bpb-us-e2.wpmucdn

.com/faculty.sites.uci.edu/dist/0/590/files/2024/01/Holman-et-al-Clinical
-Psych-Science-Online-First-87ecc6f394ba3586.pdf.

12. *NAS Exhaustive Concordance*, Bible Hub, accessed November 12, 2024,
    https://biblehub.com/hebrew/3820.htm.

13. *Vine's Complete Expository Dictionary of Old and New Testament Words*, ed.
    Merrill Unger (Nashville: Thomas Nelson, 1996), 109.

14. John Bunyan, *The Holy War Made by Shaddai upon Diabolus for the
    Regaining of the Metropolis of the World* (Boston: Thomas, 1817), 9.

15. "Music and Health: What You Need to Know," National Center for
    Complementary and Integrative Health, accessed November 12, 2024,
    www.nccih.nih.gov/health/music-and-health-what-you-need-to-know.

16. Sandra Garrido et al., "Musical Prescriptions for Mood Improvement:
    An Experimental Study," *The Arts in Psychotherapy* 51 (2016): 46–53,
    www.sciencedirect.com/science/article/abs/pii/S0197455616301071.

17. Nina Avramova, "How Music Can Change the Way You Feel and Act," CNN
    Health, updated February 20, 2019, www.cnn.com/2019/02/08/health
    /music-brain-behavior-intl/index.html.

18. Jacob Jolij and Maaike Meurs, "Music Alters Visual Perception," PLOS ONE,
    April 21, 2011, https://journals.plos.org/plosone/article?id=10.1371/journal
    .pone.0018861.

19. Craig A. Anderson and Nicholas L. Carnagey, "Exposure to Violent Media:
    The Effects of Songs with Violent Lyrics on Aggressive Thoughts and
    Feelings," *Journal of Personality and Social Psychology*, 84, no. 5 (2003):
    960–71, www.apa.org/pubs/journals/releases/psp-845960.pdf; see also
    Raymond Surette, "Performance Crime and Justice," *Current Issues in
    Criminal Justice* 27, no. 2 (2015): 195–216, www.tandfonline.com/doi/abs/10
    .1080/10345329.2015.12036041.

20. H. Bringman et al., "Relaxing Music as Pre-Medication Before Surgery: A
    Randomised Controlled Trial," *Anaesthesiologica Scandinavica* 53, no. 6
    (2009): 759–64, https://onlinelibrary.wiley.com/doi/abs/10.1111/j.1399-6576
    .2009.01969.x.

21. M. Soledad Cepeda et al., "Music for Pain Relief," *Cochrane Database of
    Systematic Reviews* 19, no. 2 (2006), https://pubmed.ncbi.nlm.nih.gov
    /16625614.

22. Jack Flynn, "18 Average Screen Time Statistics [2023]: How Much Screen

Time Is Too Much?," Zippia, March 10, 2023, www.zippia.com/advice/average-screen-time-statistics/.

23. Sudheer Kumar Muppalla et al., "Effects of Excessive Screen Time on Child Development: An Updated Review and Strategies for Management," *Cureus* 15, no. 6 (2023), www.ncbi.nlm.nih.gov/pmc/articles/PMC10353947.

## Chapter 4: The Pattern of Insecurity

1. Susan Pinker, "Does Facebook Make Us Unhappy and Unhealthy?," *Wall Street Journal*, updated May 25, 2017, www.wsj.com/articles/does-facebook-make-us-unhappy-and-unhealthy-1495729227.

2. See Max Woolf, "18+ Mobile Photography Statistics for 2024," PhotoAid, updated October 15, 2024, https://photoaid.com/blog/mobile-photography-statistics/.

3. See Denise Dador, "'Selfie Wrist' Injuries Becoming More Common, Doctor Says," ABC Eyewitness News, December 20, 2018, https://abc7.com/selfies-selfie-injury-wrist-hand/4932142/.

4. Cited in Karl Kinnel, "How Many Selfies Are Taken a Day in 2024? Facts and Statistics," Eksposure, July 22, 2022, www.eksposure.com/selfie-statistics/.

5. Michael Smith, "Studies Show That Children Just Want to Be Famous," Liberty Voice, August 3, 2013, https://guardianlv.com/2013/08/studies-show-that-children-just-want-to-be-famous/.

6. See Kendra Cherry, "How Social Comparison Theory Influences Our Views on Ourselves," Very Well Mind, updated on May 21, 2024, www.verywellmind.com/what-is-the-social-comparison-process-2795872.

7. Brian A. Feinstein et al., "Negative Social Comparison on Facebook and Depressive Symptoms: Rumination as a Mechanism," *Psychology of Popular Media Culture* 2, no. 3 (2013), 161–70, https://psycnet.apa.org/record/2013-25137-002.

8. See Jessica Brown, "Happy Couples Post Less About Their Relationships on Social Media," Indy 100, December 17, 2016, www.indy100.com/news/happy-couples-post-less-social-media-facebook-twitter-instagram-7481496.

9. Charles H. Cooley, *Human Nature and the Social Order* (New York: Scribner, 1902), 184.

## Chapter 5: The Pattern of Distraction

1. Quoted in Daniel McFadden, "You Choose," *Economist*, December 16, 2010.

2. Cited in McFadden, "You Choose."

3. Barry Schwartz, *The Paradox of Choice: Why More Is Less* (New York: Ecco, 2004), 2.

4. Neil Postman, *Amusing Ourselves to Death: Public Discourse in the Age of Show Business* (New York: Penguin, 1985).

5. Nicholas Carr, *The Shallows: What the Internet Is Doing to Our Brains* (New York: Norton, 2010), 193–94.

6. Brett McCracken, *The Wisdom Pyramid: Feeding Your Soul in a Post-Truth World* (Wheaton, IL: Crossway, 2021), 41–42, italics in original.

7. See Andrew K. Przybylski and Netta Weinstein, "Can You Connect with Me Now? How the Presence of Mobile Communication Technology Influences Face-to-Face Conversation Quality," *Journal of Social and Personal Relationships* 30, no. 3 (2013): 237–46, https://journals.sagepub.com/doi/full/10.1177/0265407512453827.

8. T. S. Eliot, "Burnt Norton," in *Four Quartets* (New York: Harcourt, Brace, 1943), 17.

9. Cited in Simon Kemp, "The Time We Spend on Social Media," Data Reportal, January 31, 2024, https://datareportal.com/reports/digital-2024-deep-dive-the-time-we-spend-on-social-media.

10. Cited in "How Much Time Do US Adults Spend Watching TV," Marketing Charts, March 31, 2023, www.marketingcharts.com/television/tv-audiences-and-consumption-229018.

11. Cited in Rebecca Moody, "Screen Time Statistics: Average Screen Time by Country," Comparitech, updated March 20, 2024, www.comparitech.com/tv-streaming/screen-time-statistics/.

12. Cited in Michael Winnick, "Putting a Finger on Our Phone Obsession," Dscout People Nerds, accessed November 12, 2024, https://dscout.com/people-nerds/mobile-touches.

13. Jeffrey M. Jones, "Church Attendance Has Declined in Most U.S. Religious Groups," Gallup, March 25, 2024, https://news.gallup.com/poll/642548/church-attendance-declined-religious-groups.aspx. This Gallup poll finds that about 44 percent of Protestant Christians attend church weekly or

almost every week, which means that 56 percent attend once a month (13 percent), seldom (27 percent), or never (16 percent). Among Catholics, the attendance figures are even lower. About 33 percent of Catholics attend church weekly or almost every week, which means that 67 percent attend once a month (17 percent), seldom (32 percent), or never (18 percent).

14. Ronald Rolheiser, *The Holy Longing: The Search for a Christian Spirituality* (New York: Doubleday, 1999), 32.

15. C. S. Lewis, *The Screwtape Letters* (New York: Macmillan, 1976), 22.

16. Lewis, *Screwtape Letters*, 66.

17. See M. G. Siegler, "Eric Schmidt: Every 2 Days We Create as Much Information as We Did Up to 2003," Tech Crunch, August 4, 2010, https://techcrunch.com/2010/08/04/schmidt-data/.

## Chapter 6: The Pattern of Offense

1. Oliver Burkeman, "The Age of Rage: Are We Really Living in Angrier Times," *The Guardian*, May 11, 2019, www.theguardian.com/lifeandstyle /2019/may/11/all-fired-up-are-we-really-living-angrier-times.

2. Susan Krauss Whitbourne, "Is Our Society Getting Increasingly Angry?," *Psychology Today*, October 12, 2010, www.psychologytoday.com/us/blog /fulfillment-any-age/201010/is-our-society-getting-increasingly-angry.

3. Sarah Lyall, "Why Is Everyone So Angry? We Investigated," *New York Times*, January 14, 2022, www.nytimes.com/2022/01/14/insider/why-is-everyone -so-angry-we-investigated.html.

4. Alvin Powell, "Soothing Advice for Mad America," *Harvard Gazette*, August 14, 2020, https://news.harvard.edu/gazette/story/2020/08/a-closer-look-at -americas-pandemic-fueled-anger.

5. Dustin Grove, "A Recent Rise in Rage: Why Are We So Angry?," WTHR, updated November 9, 2023, www.wthr.com/article/news/local/why -are-we-so-angry-indianapolis-indiana/531-5d27ad39-a540-41d1-9012 -75202da6654a.

6. Elizabeth Chang, "Americans Are Living in a Big Anger Incubator: Experts Have Tips for Regulating Our Rage," *Washington Post*, June 29, 2020, www .washingtonpost.com/lifestyle/wellness/anger-control-protests-masks -coronavirus/2020/06/29/a1e882d0-b279-11ea-8758-bfd1d045525a_story.html.

7. Charles Duhigg, "The Real Roots of American Rage," *The Atlantic*, January/

February 2019, www.theatlantic.com/magazine/archive/2019/01/charles
-duhigg-american-anger/576424/.

8. See Sarah N. Garfinkel et al., "Anger in Brain and Body: the Neural and
Physiological Perturbation of Decision-Making by Emotion," *Social
Cognitive and Affective Neuroscience* 11, no. 1 (2015): 150–58, https://pmc
.ncbi.nlm.nih.gov/articles/PMC4692323/.

9. See Amy F. T. Arnsten et al., "The Effects of Stress Exposure on Prefrontal
Cortex: Translating Basic Research into Successful Treatments for Post-
Traumatic Stress Disorder," *Neurobiology of Stress* 1 (2015): 89–99, www
.sciencedirect.com/science/article/pii/S2352289514000101.

10. Elizabeth Dougherty, "Anger Management: Scientists Probe Wrath's Nature
in the Hope of Devising Cures," *Harvard Medicine*, Summer 2011, https://
magazine.hms.harvard.edu/articles/anger-management.

11. Virgil Zeigler-Hill and Todd K. Shackelford, eds., *Encyclopedia of
Personality and Individual Differences* (Cham, Switzerland: Springer, 2020),
quoted in Jeremy Sutton, "18 Effective Thought-Stopping Techniques (& 10
PDFs)," Positive Psychology, February 2, 2024, https://positivepsychology
.com/thought-stopping-techniques/.

12. Kyle Benson, "The Anger Iceberg," Gottman Institute, updated June 26,
2024, www.gottman.com/blog/the-anger-iceberg/.

13. Stephen Covey, *The 7 Habits of Highly Effective People* (New York: Fireside,
1990), 30–31.

## Chapter 7: The Pattern of Pleasure

1. Joy Davidman, *Smoke on the Mountain* (Philadelphia: Westminster, 1954), 24.

2. Cited in Arielle Feger, "Digital Makes Up Over Three-Quarters of Total Ad
Spend in the US," eMarketer, August 27, 2024, www.emarketer.com/content
/digital-makes-up-over-three-quarters-total-ad-spend-us.

3. Jon Clifton and Julie Ray, "What's the Happiest Country on Earth," Gallup,
March 20, 2024, https://news.gallup.com/poll/612125/happiest-country
-earth.aspx.

4. Dan Witters, "U.S. Depression Rates Reach New Highs," Gallup, May 17,
2023, https://news.gallup.com/poll/505745/depression-rates-reach-new
-highs.aspx.

5. Michel Hansenne, "Valuing Happiness Is Not a Good Way of Pursuing

Happiness, but Prioritizing Positivity Is: A Replication Study," *Psychologica Belgica* 61, no. 1 (2021): 306–14, www.ncbi.nlm.nih.gov/pmc/articles /PMC8588931/.

6. Roland Zahn et al., "The Neural Basis of Human Social Values: Evidence from Functional MRI," *Cerebral Cortex* 19, no. 2 (2008): 276–83, https:// pmc.ncbi.nlm.nih.gov/articles/PMC2733324/; see also Alex Korb, "The Grateful Brain: The Neuroscience of Giving Thanks," *Psychology Today*, November 20, 2012, www.psychologytoday.com/us/blog/prefrontal-nudity /201211/the-grateful-brain.

7. Korb, "Grateful Brain."

8. Robert A. Emmons and Michael E. McCullough, "Counting Blessings Versus Burdens: An Experimental Investigation of Gratitude and Subjective Well-Being in Daily Life," *Journal of Personality and Social Psychology* 84, no. 2 (2003): 377–89, https://greatergood.berkeley.edu/pdfs/GratitudePDFs /6Emmons-BlessingsBurdens.pdf.

9. A. J. Jacobs, *Thanks a Thousand: A Gratitude Journey* (New York: TED Books/Simon & Schuster, 2018), 1–6.

## Chapter 8: The Pattern of Despair

1. Taylor Branch, *Parting the Waters: America in the King Years, 1954–63* (New York: Simon & Schuster, 1988), 143–205.

2. "Long-Term Trends in Deaths of Despair," Joint Economic Committee, September 5, 2019, www.jec.senate.gov/public/index.cfm/republicans/2019 /9/long-term-trends-in-deaths-of-despair.

3. "'Diseases of Despair' Have Soared over Past Decade in US," BMJ Open, November 10, 2020, https://blogs.bmj.com/bmjopen/2020/11/10/diseases -of-despair-have-soared-over-past-decade-in-us/.

4. "Long-Term Trends."

5. Dan Witters, "U.S. Depression Rates Reach New Highs," Gallup, May 17, 2023, https://news.gallup.com/poll/505745/depression-rates-reach-new -highs.aspx.

6. Jessica Booth, "Anxiety Statistics and Facts," *Forbes*, updated October 23, 2023, www.forbes.com/health/mind/anxiety-statistics/.

7. Matthew D. Lieberman et al., "Putting Feelings into Words: Affect Labeling

Disrupts Amygdala Activity in Response to Affective Stimuli," *Psychological Science* 18, no. 5 (2007): 421–28, https://pubmed.ncbi.nlm.nih.gov/17576282/.

8. Shiting Yuan et al., "Neural Effects of Cognitive Behavioral Therapy in Psychiatric Disorders: A Systematic Review and Activation Likelihood Estimation Meta-Analysis," *Frontiers in Psychology* 13 (2022), https://pmc.ncbi.nlm.nih.gov/articles/PMC9112423/.

9. Emma B. Jones and Louise Sharpe, "Cognitive Bias Modification: A Review of Meta-Analyses," *Journal of Affective Disorders* 223 (2017): 175–83, https://pubmed.ncbi.nlm.nih.gov/28759865/.

10. Quoted in Sterling Whitaker, "Here Are the Lyrics to Jelly Roll's 'Need a Favor,'" Taste of Country, November 8, 2023, https://tasteofcountry.com/jelly-roll-need-a-favor-lyrics/.

11. Martin Luther King Jr., *The Autobiography of Martin Luther King Jr.*, ed. Clayborne Carson (New York: Warner Books, 1998), 76.

12. "Never Alone," author unknown, tune arrangement by Baylus B. McKinney, 1895.

## Chapter 10: Think About These Things

1. Jennifer Crocker et al., "Downward Comparison, Prejudice, and Evaluations of Others: Effects of Self-Esteem and Threat," *Journal of Personality and Social Psychology* 52, no. 5 (1987): 907–16, https://pubmed.ncbi.nlm.nih.gov/3585702/.

2. See "Marriage and Couples," Gottman Institute, accessed November 12, 2024, www.gottman.com/about/research/couples/.

3. "The Sound Relationship House," Gottman Institute, accessed November 12, 2024, www.gottman.com/blog/the-sound-relationship-house-the-positive-perspective/.

4. "Way Maker," by Sinach (Osinachi Kalu Okoro-Egbu) in 2015.

5. *A Beautiful Mind* (DreamWorks, 2001), directed by Ron Howard, written by Akiva Goldsman and Sylvia Nasar, www.imdb.com/title/tt0268978/quotes/.

6. See Hanjoo Kim and Michelle G. Newman, "Worry and Rumination Enhance a Positive Emotional Contrast Based on the Framework of the Contrast Avoidance Model," *Journal of Anxiety Disorders* 94 (2023), www.ncbi.nlm.nih.gov/pmc/articles/PMC10071830/.

## Chapter 12: Win the Morning

1. M. Scott Peck, *The Road Less Traveled: A New Psychology of Love, Traditional Values, and Spiritual Growth* (New York: Touchstone, 1978). See "Most Weeks on Bestseller List," Guinness World Records, accessed November 12, 2024, www.guinnessworldrecords.com/world-records/67373-most-weeks -on-best-seller-list.

2. See Jennifer Schuessler, "Inside the List," *New York Times*, March 11, 2011, www.nytimes.com/2011/03/20/books/review/InsideList-t.html.

3. Cited in Amantha Imber, "What Super Productive People Do Differently," *Harvard Business Review*, December 8, 2020, https://hbr.org/2020/12/what -super-productive-people-do-differently.

4. See Morgan Smith, "3 Morning Habits to Help You Be Happier and More Productive at Work, According to Psychologists," CNBC, updated December 19, 2022, www.cnbc.com/2022/12/18/psychologists-morning -habits-to-help-you-be-happier-more-productive.html.

5. "Why Routines Are Good for Your Health," Piedmont, accessed November 12, 2024, www.piedmont.org/living-real-change/why-routines-are-good-for -your-health.

6. Jessica Jones, "Habits That Shape Our Daily Life," Sleep Judge, August 10, 2020, https://www.thesleepjudge.com/benefits-of-a-morning-routine/; see also Shayanne Gal and Rachel Premack, "The Dramatically Different Morning Routines of Americans at Every Income Level," *Business Insider*, June 11, 2018, www.businessinsider.com/rich-middle-class-low-income -morning-routines-2018-6.

7. Melody Wilding, "What You Can Learn from the Morning Routines of Super Productive People," *Forbes*, May 16, 2018, www.forbes.com/sites /melodywilding/2018/05/16/what-you-can-learn-from-the-morning -routines-of-productive-people/.

8. Jay Rai, "Why You Should Stop Checking Your Phone in the Morning (and What to Do Instead)," *Forbes*, April 2, 2021, www.forbes.com/sites /forbescoachescouncil/2021/04/02/why-you-should-stop-checking-your -phone-in-the-morning-and-what-to-do-instead/.

9. Rai, "Why You Should Stop."

10. Quoted in Claudia Khaw, "I Copied Steve Jobs' Morning Routine for a Week, from Diet to Outfit. Here's How It Went," Vulcan Post, October 19, 2022,

https://vulcanpost.com/805652/review-steve-jobs-apple-ceo-morning
-routine-malaysia/.

11. See "The Power of Pessimism," Einzelgänger, July 24, 2019, https://
einzelganger.co/the-power-of-pessimism/.

12. Ap Dijksterhuis and Ad van Knippenberg, "The Relation Between
Perception and Behavior, or How to Win a Game of Trivial Pursuit,"
*Journal of Personality and Social Psychology* 74, no. 4 (1998): 865–77,
www.researchgate.net/publication/13710149_The_Relation_Between
_Perception_and_Behavior_or_How_to_Win_a_Game_of_Trivial
_Pursuit.

13. Charles Spurgeon, "Memory—The Handmaid of Hope," Metropolitan
Tabernacle Pulpit, vol. 11, October 15, 1865, www.spurgeon.org/resource
-library/sermons/memory-the-handmaid-of-hope/#flipbook/.

## Chapter 13: On Things Above

1. Edward Judson, *The Life of Adoniram Judson* (New York: Ansom D. F.
Randolph, 1883), 20.

2. Ernest Becker, *The Denial of Death* (New York: Free Press, 1973).

3. James D. Knowles, *Memoir of Mrs. Ann H. Judson: Late Missionary to
Burmah* (Boston: Lincoln & Edmands, 1829), 43.